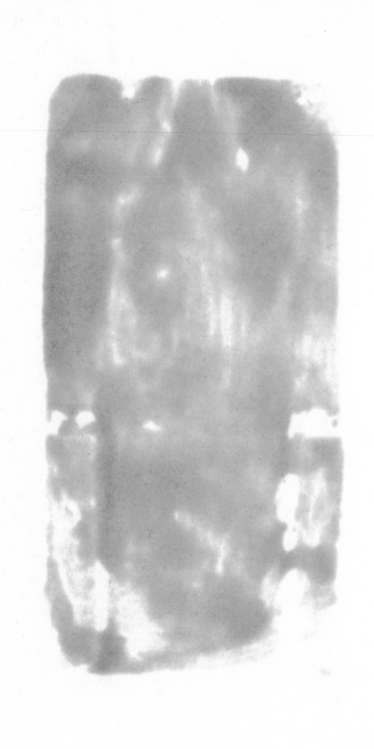

NATURAL COLLAGE

THE MAKING OF PICTURES WITH
SEEDS, LEAVES AND GRASSES

NATURAL COLLAGE

THE MAKING OF PICTURES WITH
SEEDS, LEAVES AND GRASSES

SALLY MILES

With line drawings by
Anthony Loynes

CHARLES SCRIBNER'S SONS · NEW YORK

Printed in Great Britain
Library of Congress Catalog Card Number 74-5964
ISBN 0 684-13895-6

TO

THE MEMORY OF

DORIS SULLIVAN

WITH MY THANKS

FOR HER PRACTICAL ENTHUSIASM

AND ENCOURAGEMENT

CONTENTS

Contents

Contents

ACKNOWLEDGEMENTS

I should like to thank all the people who kindly allowed me to borrow back pictures I had made and sold or given away, so that they could be photographed for inclusion in this book: Mr and Mrs Trewin Copplestone, for the loan of *The Turkey* (Plate 1), *The Alphabet* (Plate 3), and *The Egyptian Bird* (Figure 13); Mr and Mrs John Hingston, for the loan of *The Chinese Cranes* (Figure 12); Mr and Mrs Eric Learmonth, for the loan of *The Angry Bird* (Figure 10); Mr and Mrs Jack Lindsay, for the loan of *Crane, Fishing* (Plate 9); Sir Bernard and Lady Miles, for the loan of *Portrait of a Man* (Plate 6), *Cross with Head* (Plate 7) and *Star of Seeds* (Figure 2); Miss Gillian Miles, for the loan of the miniature (Figure 5); Mr and Mrs Jose Moreno, for the loan of *The Reed-Warbler* (Plate 8); the Very Rev. Martin Sullivan, Dean of St Paul's, for the loan of *Crane Triumphant* (Plate 10); Mr Sama Swaminathan, for the loan of *The Gryphon* (Figure 9); the Ven. the Archdeacon of London and Mrs Woodhouse, for the loan of *The Crested Duck* (Figure 1) and *The Hawk* (Figure 11); Mr and Mrs Adam Woolfitt, for the loan of *St George and the Dragon* (Plate 5) and the *Dragon with Flies* which is shown on the jacket.

I should also like to thank my husband and my three children, Ben and Jo and Dido, for their help, both with the making of my pictures and with the putting together of this book. Many things might have been left out had they not jogged my memory, and many pictures might never have been made had they not found some new leaf or seed or suggested some new way in which to use an already familiar one. I must thank them too for being patient when the pictures became more important than the household chores—

Sally Miles

LIST OF ILLUSTRATIONS

Colour Plates

Pictures created by Sally Miles and photographed by Adam Woolfitt

The Christmas Crib from St Paul's Cathedral, London
created by Sally Miles and photographed by David Cripps

Monochrome Half-Tones

Line Drawings and Diagrams

Drawn by Anthony Loynes

Seeds, Leaves and Seed-Containers, listed in the text:

INTRODUCTION

Since I began to make my very first picture people have asked me questions like "Whatever made you think of making pictures with leaves and seeds?", "How did you start making them?", "We've never seen anything like *these* pictures before, how do you do them?" Of course, many people do make pictures, designs and collages, from dried and preserved natural materials, but I myself have never yet seen these materials used in quite the same way as mine. The Victorians passed many a long winter's evening creating beautiful designs with dried grasses or assembling pressed flowers into intricate patterns, and other people have worked out ways of their own, but nowhere have I found leaves and seeds used as stones are used in mosaics or as stitches are used in embroidery. For me, these have become the most exciting ways of using these materials—finding the leaf or seed of the right shape and colour to build up each part of a picture.

It all started about seven years ago when we were living very close to a London park full of the most lovely plane trees. In the autumn I used to take my (then) small children for walks in the park, and as I saw them kicking their way through the great golden carpet of fallen leaves I thought 'What a waste! All these wonderful leaves with their magnificent colour—if only one could preserve them somehow instead of letting them be swept into piles and driven off in the corporation truck.' So, with the children, I collected as many perfect leaves as I could and took them home, longing to preserve and use them, but having no idea how.

We had in the house a long long entrance hall which seemed never-ending, and which I had never quite known how to decorate. One crisp sunny autumn day, shepherding the children in from a walk in the park, where they had gathered armfuls of huge leaves, I was struck by the dullness of the hall after the brightness outside. I thought how wonderful it would be to bring some of that brightness into the house—and suddenly realised that the children were clutching a way of doing just that: I would cover my walls with the golden leaves!

15

With great excitement, and a certain fear that I might ruin the walls forever, I set about sticking. All turned out well! (On pages 119–20 I have described in detail how I did it, in case you too have a large wall you don't know what to do with.)

After my success with the hall, I began to think of all the other ways I might use leaves and seeds before they fell and rotted back into the ground. I came to notice how some seeds looked like birds' eyes or claws, how some leaves looked like feathers or crests or beaks; and with this discovery there began the actual making of pictures.

I had read about the technique of preserving leaves in glycerine, and I tried this with some willow leaves from my sister's country garden. When the leaves had been dipped in the glycerine and were all laid out on a sheet of newspaper to get rid of the excess, I was struck by the lively way they curved—and suddenly I saw them as the tail-feathers of a bird. So, with some of these leaves and with some honesty, which happened to be in the house, I began my very first picture. I finished it too! It came to be called simply *BIRD* 1. (It is shown in Plate 4 on page 77.) There were many more to follow.

Soon we were to move to the country, where I was excited by the number of different leaves and seeds that were all around. I began to gather more and more materials, preserving those that needed preservation but simply storing those, the vast majority, that had dried naturally in the sun and wind. Although I had been brought up in the country, and indeed knew the name of nearly every common wild flower, I had never before looked at their leaves so closely or noticed the intricate and subtle design of their heads.

I gathered more and more, storing each different kind of seed and leaf separately, in anything from old match-boxes to shoe-boxes and carrier bags. In no time at all my stocks filled an old chest of drawers (to say nothing of what was being pressed under every carpet in the house) and we decided it would be best to buy a large greenhouse and butt it onto the house, like a conservatory, and put all the materials, and me, in there together. My picture-making had begun in earnest.

Exhibitions and commissions quickly followed—and not commissions for pictures only, for I was also invited to design and make some large panels to decorate the windows of a London store—Simpson of Piccadilly—and, most exciting of all, to create a new Christmas Crib for St Paul's Cathedral. Making the panels for the store and the three-dimensional figures for the Crib involved

Figure 1 The duck's crest is made of Spanish seeds, dried to a pale gold colour, which are favourites of mine because their lustrous shimmer is like the play of light on living feathers. The neck is of deeper gold hogweed seeds, the wing of glycerined willow leaves – a darkish olive green – growing from arcs of ash "wings" (the "wing" from the ash seed-container is one of the materials I use most frequently). I used split bleached aspidistra leaves for his tail, and pale downy pampas grass for his breast. His eye is the disc from a poppy seed-head, surrounded by the dark green of shrub honeysuckle leaf; his webbed feet are brown palm spikes interspersed with willow. I worked at this picture in spurts of about an hour – the fits-and-starts method works perfectly well! – and it took me about a week to complete.

me in extending and developing the techniques I had acquired, and also in widening the range of my materials. I have written about this in more detail in Chapter 6, and in Chapter 7 I have described some work done by children; but in the earlier chapters I have talked about the materials and the equipment I use, and about the designing, making and framing of the pictures themselves. I am sure that anyone who experiments with the making of pictures from natural materials will evolve methods of his or her own and find tools he or she cannot do without; I am generally faithful to Copydex, for instance, a latex-based adhesive which I have found excellent for sticking the seeds, grasses and so on to the fabric backing, but if you cannot get Copydex—it isn't, for example, available in the United States—don't despair, experiment with alternative brands (Sobo is an American possibility, though I have not yet tried it myself) until you find one that suits you. All that matters is that the tools, the equipment, the techniques, should work for you; the ones I describe here are simply those that work for me, just as the designs I have used and the materials I have collected have been those that caught my own imagination.

SALLY MILES
Essex, 1972

MATERIALS

Before i began to make pictures from seeds there was nothing I enjoyed more than going for a walk, but my enjoyment was always marred by the thought of all the household chores I ought to be doing instead—washing up, making the beds, even sewing on all those buttons that children seem to lose from every garment they possess. But now, if the weather is at all possible, friends have only to hint at an outing, and there I am, ready with carrier bags and match-boxes, before the words are out of their mouths. Beds are left unmade, washing up is left undone, safety pins remain excellent substitutes for buttons, as I spend hours and hours tramping down bridle paths and clambering across ditches, collecting my "palette"!

In the early days the children became just as keen as I was, and tried to outdo each other in the number of different varieties of seeds they could find, often persuading me to walk just a little further "in case there's one more kind". Now, however, their excitement has somewhat waned, and an enquiry about my whereabouts was met one day with a superior "Mummy? Oh, I suppose she's scrabbling in the hedgerows again"! I am just as bad in the town, looking hopefully along the pavements for leaves and seeds.

One of the most important lessons I have learned about collecting materials is "Pick it when you see it". If you come across something you may be able to use, gather it immediately; it may take ages to find exactly the same thing again— indeed, the chances are you may *never* do so, for one of the wonderful things about these natural materials, as opposed to man-made artist's materials like paints, is that no two items are identical: no two willow leaves have exactly the same curve, no two ash wings quite the same twist.

Another lesson is "Watch the seasons and think ahead". Very often a particular leaf or seed can be gathered at only one season of the year. Once that season is over, you will have to wait for months before Nature provides you with any more. This can be very awkward if you find that you have run out of, say, hogweed, as I once did while doing a picture in October—I had to wait until the following August to finish it! Of course, if you live in the south you may have another chance and by taking a journey north, where the seasons are usually anything up to a month behind, you may, with luck, find the seed you need without having to wait until the next year.

Gathering materials on country walks is only one way to build up your stock. If you are a keen gardener you can grow your own—there are many different ornamental grasses and everlasting flowers which are suitable. It is a good idea to save a few seeds from each packet (this applies to vegetables as well—parsnips, lettuce, turnips and so on), as these may well keep you going until your own crop has gone to seed.

But picture-making with natural materials is not just a country activity: the town has its own opportunities to offer. Town parks and gardens are often stocked with plants not easily found in the country. So, if you live in a town flat or have no garden of your own, don't feel that making pictures with natural materials is something you won't be able to do. You may not have the country-side to choose your materials from, but you can build up a quite different and exciting "palette" from town parks and pavements. If you see some exciting leaves or seeds in a stranger's garden, never be afraid to knock on the door and ask if you can collect some. People always seem to be delighted to help, and take a great interest when you explain why you want the seeds.

If for some reason you cannot get out to parks or gardens, and there is no one who can collect materials for you, you can, of course, buy your own. When I look at the colourful packets of flower seeds and vegetable seeds arranged in rows in the shops, I long for some seedsman to market packets with see-through windows, so that I can tell what the seeds themselves look like. You can imagine the sort of reaction I get from puzzled salesmen as I gently shake and feel an unfamiliar packet, trying to judge the shape and size of its contents! Out of season, packets of seeds can be ordered by post from the well-known firms. Florists' shops too can be a very useful, if somewhat expensive, source of interesting material, especially those which sell imported dried and preserved flowers and grasses.

Something I have started to do only recently, but wish I had begun earlier, is to make a sort of catalogue of all the seeds and other materials I have used. I have a large scrap-book, and into this I put a specimen of each kind of material I use in my pictures. I stick the specimen with adhesive to the left-hand side of the page, and opposite it I note not only what it is, but also how I came by it, what pictures I use it in, and so on.

One of the incidental, but very important, pleasures of this craft is the making of new acquaintances and friendships. Sometimes people who have seen my pictures on display at exhibitions or in private houses have come up to me and introduced themselves, and offered me envelopes, match-boxes, or even poly-thene bags full of seeds they have found on holidays abroad. Small, but greatly treasured, packages come through the post, often containing some rare or special grass-head which I have never seen before. A simple unfamiliar seed or leaf can be the inspiration for a whole new series of pictures.

When collecting, make sure you always have something with you in which to carry your treasure home. Many's the time I have gone out unprepared—without so much as the odd pocket on me—and come across a wealth of some exciting seed. I remember once discovering some beautiful poppy heads; finding I had nothing else to put them in, I took off my shoes, filled them, and walked home barefoot!

Carrier bags I find best for this job of harvesting. If you try using a basket, you very often lose seeds through the open-work. A carrier bag can be stuffed into your pocket or under your belt until the moment you need it—and it is light to carry home, even brimming full. Plastic ones are best as if it starts to rain they don't get soaked through and break. There is nothing worse than putting a paper bag down on a wet bank while you become absorbed in gathering some new leaf —and then see the bottom fall out when you pick it up again!

Another piece of equipment which can be useful is a walking stick. Just as the best and juiciest blackberries are always the least accessible, so the finest clusters of ash seeds hang waiting to be gathered—just out of reach. If you have a walking stick with a good curved handle, you can loop it over the bough, pull it gently towards you, and gather those perfect seeds or leaves. You will find, too, that a penknife or an old kitchen knife or, better still, a small pair of secateurs is useful for cutting those stubborn stems. Last of all, *stout* shoes or boots, which will make it possible for you to clamber across ditches or plough your way through muddy fields to reach reeds or grasses growing by streams or in marshland.

Once you are armed with your carrier bag, walking stick, penknife and boots, collecting becomes easy—you may well find it to be one of the most enjoyable parts of this business of picture-making. Just about everything and anything can be used in one way or another, and you never know what you will find next—or where. I remember how when I was having my last baby in hospital I was given a beautiful bouquet with some unusually small sprigs of eucalyptus. The nurses were appalled when I stripped off the eucalyptus leaves, put them in an envelope, and gave this to my husband with instructions to put them under the carpet the moment he got home!

Particularly Useful Materials

There are about forty materials which I find especially useful and which I like to keep in stock in my store. Among the wild flower leaves, the ones that I probably use most are silverweed, pineapple weed, carline thistle and grass-wrack pondweed. I also use a good many wild flower seeds and seed-pods, and here my favourites are hogweed, wild carrot, cow parsley, wild angelica, wild poppies, sorrel and plantain. I collect a good many leaves from trees and shrubs, especially sea buckthorn, shrub honeysuckle, monkey puzzle, pine and yew and juniper, the willows, and magnolia. Some of the tree seeds and seed-containers are also very useful, particularly those of sycamore, maple, elm and my great stand-by, ash. There seem to be so many marvellous varieties of ferns and reeds and grasses that it is difficult to pick out a few, but the ones I think I use most are wood small-reed, wild oat, the quaking grasses, creeping brown sedge and lesser pond sedge, velvet bent, wood millet, the meadow grasses, pampas grass, bracken and lady fern. Among the seeds and pods of the cultivated flowers I like to keep in stock are honesty, globe thistle, poppy, lupin and sunflower. I also use vegetable seeds—parsnip, lettuce and turnip especially—and a number of miscellaneous items, including split peas, lentils and melon seeds.

Because I find these particular materials so useful, I have written a short passage of description about each. In the majority of cases these descriptions are illustrated by line drawings, showing the seed or leaf or seed-head drawn to what is, roughly speaking, the actual size of specimens in my store; this may make it easier to visualize working with them.

Wild Flower Leaves

I used to collect wild flowers but barely noticed their lovely leaves; nowadays, though, I see beautiful specimens everywhere, in town and country alike, on banks, in parks, on wasteland—even on the daisies in the grass!

SILVERWEED POTENTILLA ANSERINA

SILVERWEED: *Potentilla Anserina*

Silverweed is useful in picture-making because of the shape and colour of its leaf. The leaf is pinnate—that is to say, it is made up of leaflets arranged in pairs on opposite sides of the stalk—and each leaflet has a sharply serrated edge. The underside of the leaf is, as the name suggests, silvery-coloured, and it has a silky texture. This silvery colour and silkiness are usually retained very well when the leaf is pressed—if anything, it is the green on the upper side of the leaf that fades. The silvery flickering appearance is unlike any other leaf I have encountered. I make great use of silverweed leaves for feathers: the tail of the turkey in Plate 1, for example, on page 65, has silverweed leaves alternating with grass-heads, and more silverweed leaves fan out as his topmost tail-feathers.

Silverweed grows almost everywhere in Britain, particularly along sandy and stony tracks. You can find larger specimens growing in pastureland, but the silvery colour is often more pronounced in smaller plants growing in drier, more barren places. In high summer the plant bears a yellow flower, rather like a buttercup's.

23

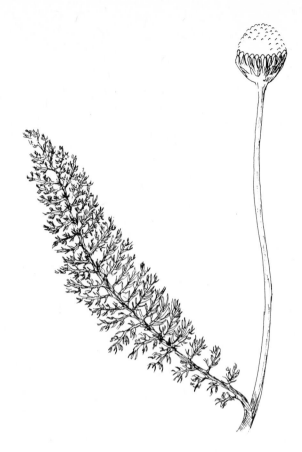

PINEAPPLE WEED
MATRICARIA MATRICARIOIDES

PINEAPPLE WEED: *Matricaria matricarioides*
Pineapple weed grows commonly on sandy tracks and in waste places. In summer it bears a yellow conical flower has which virtually no petals, with a strong fragrance when crushed.

The leaves may be gathered at any time during the summer. They are arranged like feathers with a mass of tiny leaflets on either side of the leaf-stalk and must be pressed very carefully so that these are not overlapping and don't get bent. (*Matricaria matricarioides* has denser, more feathery leaves than other varieties.) When dry, they are a greyish colour. I use them whole in some pictures; in others, I work with the separate leaflets. Don't pluck the leaflets from the leaf-stalk until you are actually assembling the picture, though.

24

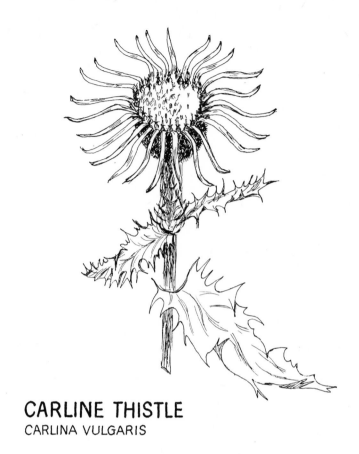

CARLINE THISTLE
CARLINA VULGARIS

CARLINE THISTLE: *Carlina vulgaris*

The carline thistle can be found in meadow and pastureland over much of the country. It is useful in picture-making because of the pale silvery-straw colour and satiny texture of its "petals" (technically speaking, these are not petals at all, but "inner bracts", a bract being a modified leaf). These "petals" are shiny, hard, and fairly stiff, with pointed ends. They are arranged in a flat ring. Each individual "petal" should be carefully removed from the head: use tweezers for this, and grip the base of the "petal"—if you try giving the tip a peremptory tweak, you will succeed only in breaking it.

I used these thistle-heads in their entirety—the flat, formal, shiny ring—to decorate the gifts of the First and Third Kings in the Crib.

25

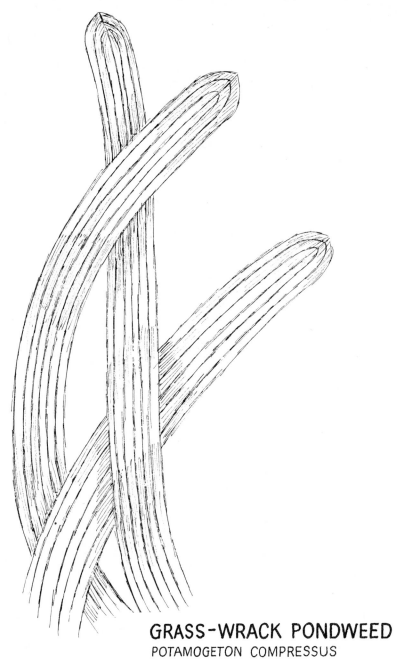

GRASS-WRACK PONDWEED
POTAMOGETON COMPRESSUS

GRASS-WRACK PONDWEED: *Potamogeton compressus*

Grass-wrack pondweed is a common pondweed which has very long, narrow leaves, a light green in colour, with rounded ends. These leaves are fairly tough and since their width is constant for almost the full length of the leaf, they are particularly useful if you want to achieve a strap-like effect in a larger picture.

Pressing these leaves is not, however, easy, simply because they are so long. It is possible to improvise a special pondweed press with two planks and piles of books given patience and sufficient space; failing that, it is probably best to put them under the spare room carpet.

Wild Flower Seeds and Pods

When you are out collecting seeds, don't just go for the obvious ones which, like hogweed, virtually flaunt their seed-heads at you. A number of flowers, such as the poppy or the lupin, hide their seeds in a special seed-container. Don't ignore these containers themselves; they can have a beauty of their own—intricate shapes, subtle colours. When I made the Boy Shepherd for the St Paul's Crib, I covered his head with tightly curling lupin seed-pods—they were perfect for the purpose. Examine, too, pips inside berries—but be *very* careful to keep them away from children.

HOGWEED: *Heracleum Sphondylium*

Hogweed belongs to the *Umbelliferae* family: a family of plants bearing flat-topped clusters of flowers whose foot-stalks are of pretty equal lengths and radiate like the ribs of an umbrella. Many other members of this family can also be used —a number of them are described on the next page; the difference between them is mainly one of size.

Hogweed is common everywhere in Britain, and flowers from June to September. From July onwards you will generally find some which has gone to seed. Don't gather the heads while the seeds are green and fleshy, as they will only shrivel and be useless (though I successfully used hogweed which was not quite ripe for St George's armour in Plate 5 on page 81); wait until they are dry and fall easily from the plant, even though they may still be slightly green. The longer you leave them to dry in the sun and wind, the more golden they will become, which makes it possible to vary the colours of the seeds one collects.

27

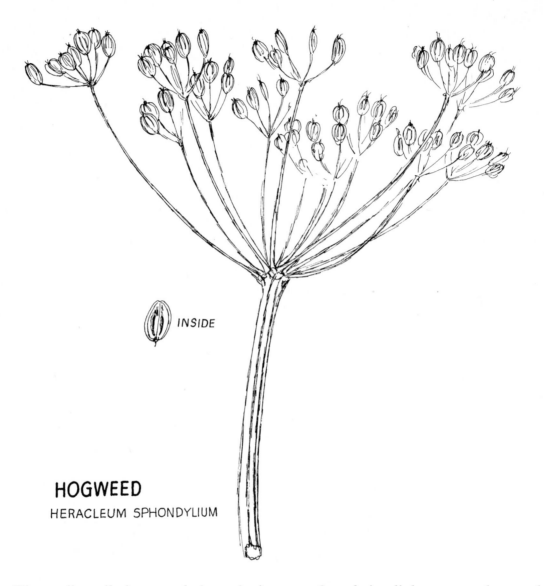

INSIDE

HOGWEED
HERACLEUM SPHONDYLIUM

They split easily into two halves, the inner surfaces being lighter, smoother, and more clearly marked.

WILD CARROT: *Daucus Carota*
COW PARSLEY: *Anthriscus sylvestris*
WILD ANGELICA: *Angelica sylvestris*

Like hogweed, wild carrot, cow parsley and wild angelica all belong to the

28

Umbelliferae family: they are, however, smaller and more delicate.

The fruits, or seeds, of the cow parsley are oblong and smoother than those of the wild carrot or the wild angelica, with less of a flange or wing; the wild angelica, which grows in wet places, bears fruit with quite a pronounced wing; while the wild carrot, which grows by the sea or on chalk, bears its "umbrella" of flowers on stalks tending to curve upward and inward, so that they need to be gently disentangled before you can extricate the seeds.

As with hogweed, you should make sure that the seeds are ripe and dry before you gather them. Look out for variations in colour—pretty reddish-brown veinings are not uncommon.

COMMON RED POPPY: *Papaver Rhoeas*
LONG SMOOTH-HEADED POPPY: *Papaver dubium*
OPIUM POPPY: *Papaver somniferum*

Modern weed-killers are so effective these days that one rarely sees the common red poppy growing amongst the crops as it used to do. However, it is, thankfully, still abundant under the hedges and along the roadside verges, and in high summer more than one stretch of road near my home is splashed with vivid scarlet along its borders. Spectacular as the colour is, however, it is not the flower petals I am after.

From August, all through autumn, until the end of the year I visit my poppy patch to gather the seed-capsules. The rounded cup of seed with its flat lid has been hardening, and the seed within ripening, since the petals wilted and shrivelled; when it is reasonably dry, I cut it from its stem and very carefully slice off the "lid", making my cut a little below the lid itself in order to avoid damaging it. I do this on the spot because I like to scatter the seed where the parent plant was growing, to make some contribution towards next year's crop (this poppy is, of course, an annual). Unless you want to use the complete capsule, it is important to wait until it is dry before cutting off the lid; if you try to gather it while it is still green and soft, the lid will buckle and shrivel as it dries, and will be useless.

I am careful to pick out seed-capsules which have undamaged and symmetrically marked lids, although I am also always on the look-out for those freaks of Nature and unique malformations which might have a character and charm all their own, and therefore a particular value, giving a picture a touch of natural individuality and even suggesting new compositions.

29

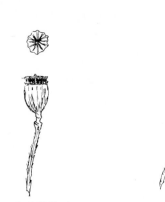

COMMON POPPY
PAPAVER RHOEAS

LONG SMOOTH-HEADED POPPY
PAPAVER DUBIUM

OPIUM POPPY
PAPAVER SOMNIFERUM

Once I have gathered the seed capsule, cut off the lid, and scattered the seed, I trim the underneath of the lid so that it will lie quite flat. Apart from a careful brush with a fine stiffish paint brush, that is all the treatment it will need, and it can be stored ready for use.

These discs, with their darker raised lines radiating from the centre, can be used complete or cut into sections. They are particularly useful when assembling abstract patterns, but they also make splendid eyes (as in Fig. 3, on page 61), birds' crests, and fins and tails for fish.

Several other poppies grow wild in Britain, each with its own differently shaped seed-heads; notable among them are the long smooth-headed poppy and the opium poppy. The former has a small elongated capsule with a slightly conical "lid", while the latter has a larger plump round capsule and a "lid" which overlaps all round like the eaves of a roof.

The long poppy has the common scarlet petals, but the opium poppy is white or pinkish mauve and is not native to Britain, being known as a "weed of cultivation".

COMMON SORREL: *Rumex Acetosa*

Common sorrel is the *Rumex* I find I have used most; others are *Rumex crispus*—the curled dock—and *Rumex hydrolapathum*—the great water dock, which is perhaps rather less common than the other two, and which grows, as its name suggests, by pools and canals. In late summer, these plants produce seed in clusters around the stem, each seed being held in a tiny winged or flanged container. The colours vary all through the season, from greenish with a pink tinge

COMMON SORREL
RUMEX ACETOSA

at the edges of the "wings" to a deep chestnut. They are not the easiest of seeds to handle being small and, perhaps more awkward, chunky, but can be very effective arranged in groups on top of larger, less interesting materials, and well worth the trouble taken.

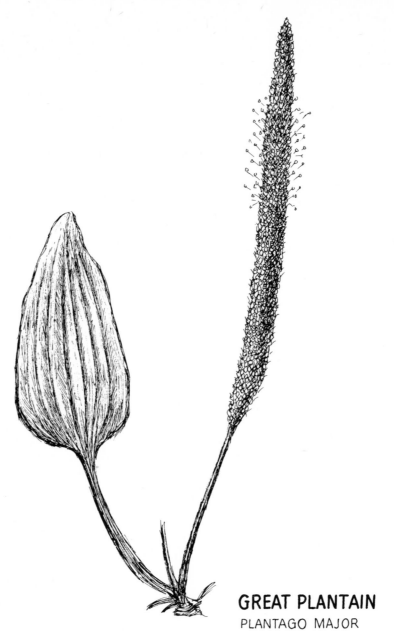

GREAT PLANTAIN
PLANTAGO MAJOR

GREAT PLANTAIN: *Plantago major*

The plantains are very common in Britain: in grassland, on roadside verges, in gardens, and often in lawns. I pick the long stalk with its seeds clustering around it once they are fairly hard and can be rubbed off without much difficulty. They are small seeds, irregularly rounded, and I either use them as individual "accents" or mass them together.

Tree Leaves and Shrub Leaves

The best leaves to use are those which are not too fleshy, as a leaf which has a good deal of juice in it can be difficult to handle, takes longer to press, and, unless you are an expert, tends to shrivel up, like skin which has been soaking too long in the bath. Don't concentrate on woods, parks and hedges so hard that you overlook the garden: soft fruit bushes can have beautiful leaves—the underside of a raspberry leaf, for instance, has a superb silveriness. Look at your indoor plants too. People make fun of aspidistra, but I have used split bleached aspidistra leaves in some of my favourite work—and literally thousands in the angels for the St Paul's Crib.

SEA BUCKTHORN
HIPPOPHAE RHAMNOIDES

SEA BUCKTHORN: *Hippophae rhamnoides*

Sea buckthorn is the willow-like thorny shrub with silvery blue-green leaves, narrow and pointed, which flourishes on sandy soil by the sea. The leaves are tough, which makes them easy to press, and their shape and colour make them particularly useful. As with most leaves, the underside is a different shade from the upper surface, a variation which makes it possible to achieve very subtle effects. Try gathering leaves at different stages of growth, from mid-May onwards—but mind the sharp spines! In fact, while you are at it, collect a few of the longer spines or thorns too. In autumn the shrub is loaded with orange berries.

33

SHRUB HONEYSUCKLE
LONICERA NITIDA

SHRUB HONEYSUCKLE: *Lonicera nitida*

Nothing like the twining honeysuckle with those heavily scented orchid-like flowers, *Lonicera nitida* is an evergreen shrub commonly used for hedging. Its leaves have the same texture as privet, but are dark green and tiny, arranged on either side of a stem, and in some ways resembling those of the herring-bone cotoneaster (*horizontalis*), though more ovate in shape. The underside of the leaf is lighter and has a purplish tinge, especially when gathered young, which is accentuated by pressing and drying.

I have used the leaves of shrub honeysuckle in several pictures as a ground, arranging them so that they overlap one another and getting in as much variety of tone as possible—some younger leaves, some more mature, some showing the upper side, some the underneath; they have a peculiar, almost iridescent quality, and the final effect somewhat resembles snakeskin. My best example is probably the Cross which appears in Plate 7 on page 89; the arms are composed of shrub honeysuckle leaves, arranged in just this way.

34

MONKEY PUZZLE
ARAUCARIA ARAUCANA

MONKEY PUZZLE: *Araucaria araucana*

This strange gaunt tree, somehow so alien to the English garden and yet so admired by the Victorians, provides unique material: the overlapping spear-shaped spikes of which its branches are composed. You cannot pick the living spikes without damaging the tree, but you may well find a small broken-off piece of branch lying on the ground. If this is already dead and old, the spikes will have lost their dark bluish-green and turned brown. When I need some monkey puzzle, I usually dash round to the local rectory, where the lawn is carpeted with fallen spikes.

These spikes are hard and fibrous—almost woody. The points are needle-sharp, and to run one under your nail is excruciatingly painful, so take care when fishing them out of store. They usually need to be trimmed at the base, and can be cleaned and polished till they gleam.

I use monkey puzzle mostly for beaks—the Crested Duck in Figure 1 on page 17 is just one example.

35

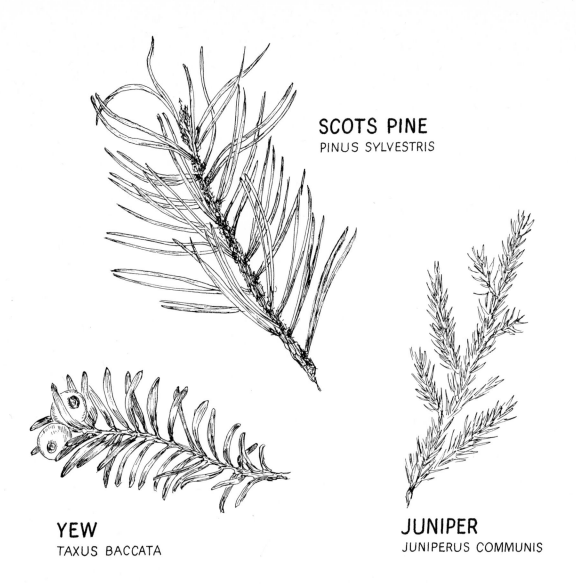

SCOTS PINE
PINUS SYLVESTRIS

YEW
TAXUS BACCATA

JUNIPER
JUNIPERUS COMMUNIS

PINE: *Pinus*

YEW: *Taxus*

JUNIPER: *Juniperus*

There are, of course, many different types of pine growing in Britain, and they produce a considerable variety of leaf and needle. Sadly, however, it is impossible —at least, in my experience—to retain the beautiful smoky blue or deep green of the living leaf once it has been dried. At least, though, the colours of the dried needles do vary, even if this variation is only in the colour range from light tan to dark chestnut. Occasionally you may find a dried needle which has retained a greenish tinge, but don't rely on this lasting as long as the picture should do—especially if it is hung in direct sunlight, which will cause any green to fade.

Dried pine needles have a great many uses in picture-making, so collect plenty. Look out for specimens with interesting curves or other distinguishing idiosyncrasies; such a feature may often suggest a new design.

Yew leaves, which turn a rich brown, are especially easy to use because they are flat, like tiny straps.

Juniper does grow wild, on chalk and limestone, but the variety I have used is the cultivated one. Like pine, juniper needles turn brown as they are dried. They are smaller and finer than yew leaves or pine needles, and this makes them more adaptable: I have used them, for instance, to create spiky crests for imaginary, heraldic-looking birds and, on the other hand, have packed them together, as close as tapestry stitches, to build up the legs of one of my from-the-life bird portraits.

WHITE WILLOW: *Salix alba*
CRACK WILLOW: *Salix fragilis*
COMMON OSIER: *Salix viminalis*

White willow, crack willow and common osier all grow in wet places, by ponds and streams and in fenny land, and have narrow pointed longish leaves. I think I probably use willow leaves more than any other, especially in my bird pictures —for beaks and claws, for wings and tails and crests. I have a particular fondness for them because it was the sight of some glycerined willow leaves that led me to make my first-ever picture.

Willow leaves are fairly tough and respond very well to drying and to pressing and to the glycerine treatment which is described on pages 59–60—this generally turns them a darkish olive green. They sometimes have a distinctive twist or flick at the end which will give a marvellous vitality to any picture in which they are set.

The leaves of the white willow are silvery grey and silky; those of the crack willow and the common osier are green, but vary slightly in shade according to the age of the leaf. All are lighter on the underside than on the upper, which can be useful in varying shades in a picture.

I used white willow in the small round picture shown on page 77; crack willow for the tail-feathers of the pair of Chinese cranes, shown in Figure 12 on page 104; and common osier in the upper part of the turkey's wing, in Plate 1 on page 65. The long pliant shoots of the common osier are used in basket-making —one of the purposes for which it is cultivated—and I hope to find a use for these in one of my three-dimensional figures.

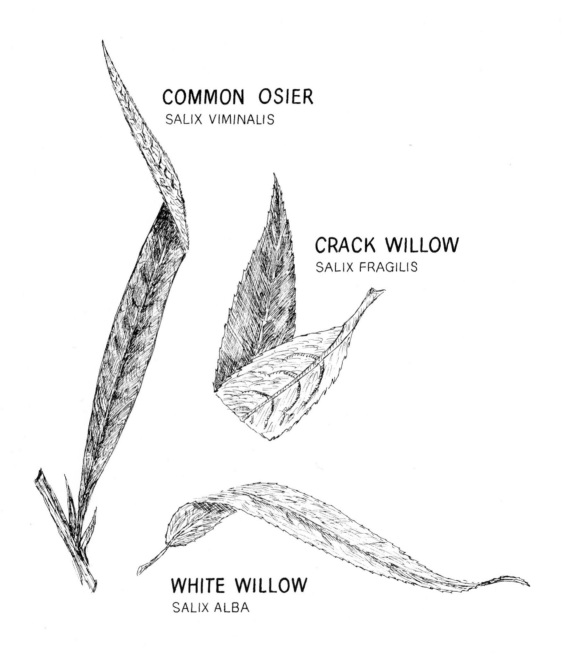

COMMON OSIER
SALIX VIMINALIS

CRACK WILLOW
SALIX FRAGILIS

WHITE WILLOW
SALIX ALBA

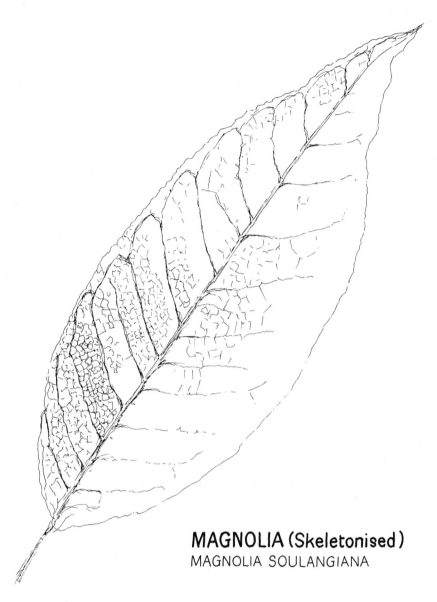

MAGNOLIA (Skeletonised)
MAGNOLIA SOULANGIANA

MAGNOLIA: *Magnolia soulangiana*
I use magnolia leaves only when skeletonised (the process is described on pages 63–4), choosing well-developed leaves which are not damaged in any way and which will lie almost, if not completely, flat. One appears in Figure 3 on page 61.

Tree Seeds

Tree seeds are generally housed in a seed-case, which often has a wing, and these can be very useful in picture-making; sycamore and ash, for instance, are very valuable. I have also used bulkier seeds, such as acorns, and am at present trying to make a rosary of oak-apples.

SYCAMORE: *Acer pseudoplatanus*
NORWAY MAPLE: *Acer platanoides*
COMMON MAPLE: *Acer campestre*

Sycamore, Norway maple and common maple all produce the familiar tadpole-shaped winged seed-cases—the kind that boys play "spinners" with—which always occur in pairs, Siamese twins joined at the seed end. In the case of sycamore, they join at a fairly narrow angle; in the common maple and the Norway maple, at an angle of 180°—in other words, the paired seeds are virtually in a straight line.

The seeds of the sycamore and the maples are rather more difficult to use than those of, say, the ash (described on page 42), since they are woody and round, almost like cherry stones, and cannot easily be extracted from their cases. The wings, however, with the pronounced spine along the top and the delicate veining of the membrane, not to mention the colour variations of pinkish and greenish beige, often very subtle, can be used in, and may indeed suggest, many different designs.

ENGLISH ELM: *Ulmus procera*
WYCH ELM: *Ulmus glabra*

The seeds of the English elm and the wych elm are very small, but are entirely surrounded by a delicate papery wing about half an inch (about 12 mm) across. The clusters are best gathered in the middle of autumn.

Elm seeds sometimes hang on the tree until well into the following year, and if protected by other vegetation may well remain undamaged. I once had the good luck to find a cluster of old seeds which had been naturally "skeletonized". The small seeds were surrounded by a most delicate tracery of veins. With a great deal of care, patience and some luck, you may succeed in skeletonizing (page 63) some elm seeds yourself. It is well worth trying to do so if you come across some well-developed seeds with good wings which have strong, clearly defined veins.

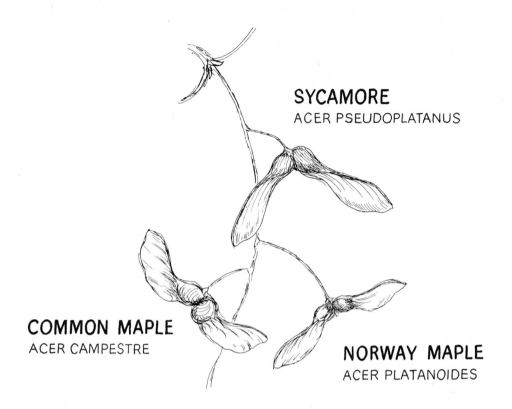

SYCAMORE
ACER PSEUDOPLATANUS

COMMON MAPLE
ACER CAMPESTRE

NORWAY MAPLE
ACER PLATANOIDES

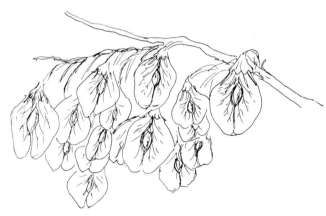

ELM
ULMUS GLABRA ULMUS PROCERA

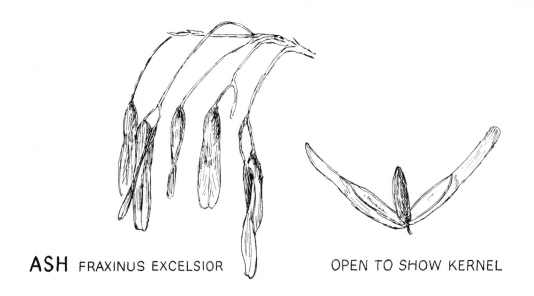

ASH FRAXINUS EXCELSIOR   OPEN TO SHOW KERNEL

ASH: *Fraxinus excelsior*

The fruit of the ash tree is one of my favourites. It is enclosed in a capsule which, like the sycamore and maple, is extended at one end into a wing. These capsules hang in bunches from the tree, developing all through the summer from their early bright green softness to the brownish hardness of autumn, tending to remain on the tree until well into the following year—in winter months, when the branches are leafless, they can be clearly seen. It is best to gather them in late autumn or early winter, when they will be quite hard and not susceptible to shrivelling, on the one hand, but not yet damaged by the weather, on the other.

The ash fruit has many uses—or rather, its different parts can be used in distinctive ways. The seed itself, which lies inside the lower part of the capsule and which can be easily removed by cracking the capsule or splitting it open, is flattish and oval, with a rich brown colour and a soft nut-like consistency (it can be easily sliced, if necessary, to thin it down a little). The wing part of the capsule is rounded at the end, with a distinct notch in the middle so that some of the wings are almost heart-shaped. If the thick part of the capsule, which holds the seed, is cut off, the wing which is left is quite flat, and can be used in a picture so that it overlaps another. A complete capsule often has a twist along its length so that if one end is held flat, the other sticks up; and when many such twisted capsules are arranged together, a very interesting rough texture may be achieved.

42

You can get different effects depending on which end of the capsule you choose to fasten down. Figure 14 on page 115 illustrates this.

I use a great deal of ash—sometimes the seeds, sometimes the seed-case (either in the natural golden colour of autumn, or bleached). The hair, beard and eyebrows of the portrait head shown in Plate 6 on page 85 are composed of ash seeds; the shoulder and wing of the dragon on the jacket are of unbleached ash seed-cases; and the body of the peacock (Plate 2, page 69) and the wings of the cranes (Plates 9 and 10, pages 100 and 101) are also of ash seed-cases, but in both these cases I used bleached ones.

It is well worth experimenting with this flexible and useful material!

Ferns, Reeds and Grasses
There are far too many useful ferns, reeds and grasses for me to attempt more than the sketchiest of lists. Wherever you go you can find new varieties, especially of grasses—indeed, you can grow your own. Grass blades are particularly useful, the blades varying, as they do, in shape and thickness—though they do tend to lose their colour when pressed, generally fading to a soft greeny-brown. Many florists' shops stock cultivated ferns and grasses—including stocks from abroad—which can help you to vary your palette.

When creating the three-dimensional figures for the St Paul's Crib I used one particular kind of reed which gave me the fright of my life. After the first Christmas that the Crib had been on display, the figures were carried up to a store-room on the Whispering Gallery level—quite a performance—and locked away securely; I sighed with relief, thinking they were safe for the next eleven months—and then a kind botanical expert telephoned me to say how beautiful the Crib was, but by the way did I realize that those reeds housed a weevil which would now be nibbling away? In great alarm I rang the Natural History Museum, and saucers of a special preventive crystal are now scattered around the store-room; that was three years ago, and all seems well.

WOOD SMALL-REED: *Calamagrostis epigejos*
Wood small-reed is, in fact, a grass, which grows in damp woodland areas and fenland. I gather this, and similar grasses, when the seeds are formed but not yet too loose. Store them on the stem, and cut off a small clump when you need it. The small seeds or florets are themselves made up of several parts (the lemma, palea, awn and so on), as well as being part of a group of seeds or florets on a

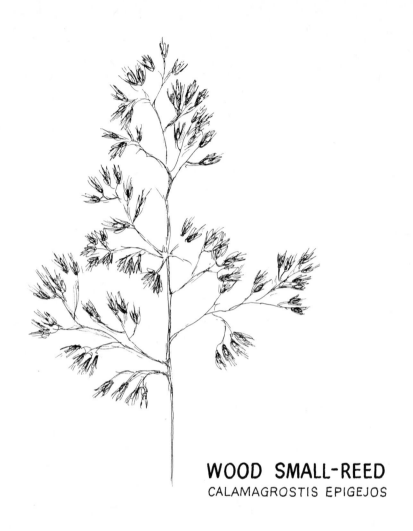

WOOD SMALL-REED
CALAMAGROSTIS EPIGEJOS

stalklet which is itself part of a group of stalklets attached to the stem—separate them carefully to see just what there is you can use. *As with all grasses*, it is sensible to take the florets apart and then re-assemble them with a little adhesive, since if you only fasten the outside of the floret into place in the picture, the inner parts may well detach themselves in time and fall out.

COMMON WILD OAT: *Avena fatua*
The common wild oat grows as a weed on arable land and waste land. The floret is relatively large, as grasses go, and the awns—little bristles or spikes—are sharply bent, sometimes to an angle of 90°, and look rather like the legs of a

44

spider. I have used the complete floret to represent an insect, just adding a couple of black lupin seed eyes, and have also peeled off the shimmering pale-gold-to-silver shuck to expose the strangely spiralling furry-based centre awn—starring the peacock's tail in Plate 2, on page 69. Try gathering the wild oats at different stages of their development; dry them by hanging them up in bunches.

WILD OAT
AVENA FATUA

COMMON QUAKING GRASS: *Briza media*

LESSER QUAKING GRASS: *Briza minor*

Common quaking grass and lesser quaking grass are quite extraordinary crea-
tions and I like always to have one or two good specimens by me. They are
similar in appearance, with beautifully arranged florets, like little hearts, dancing
and quivering on thread-like wiry stalklets. The former is perennial and grows
on chalky pasture, the latter an annual which can be found along roadsides and
on farmland (most commonly in south-west England), and which has flattish
"packets" of seed rather broader than those of its common cousin. These seeds
are rather chunky, and one should take care when picture-making to provide
enough room for them between the background and the glass, and to glue each
little segment individually to the backing.

QUAKING GRASS
BRIZA

CREEPING BROWN SEDGE
CAREX DISTICHA

CREEPING BROWN SEDGE: *Carex disticha*

Some grass seed-complexes or florets can be used entire or separated into their various parts, like the wild oat (page 44–5); some I use only in their entirety, like the quaking grass (though I do sometimes take off the bottom few segments to get the exact size I want); and some I always separate into parts which can then be used individually, as I do with this grass—or more correctly, this sedge—which grows in wet places.

The seeds of the creeping brown sedge are a useful dark brown colour, and can be used in combination with lighter-coloured seeds of a similar size to make interesting patterns and textures. They combine well, for example, with lettuce seeds.

Like all grass seeds, they are particularly useful for miniature work, being small and delicate.

LESSER POND SEDGE: *Carex acutiformis*

Lesser pond sedge grows by ponds and canals. It is much less shaggy than the creeping brown sedge, and the individual seeds or fruits are rather more chunky. They grow packed closely together, clustered round a stem, rather in the manner of a plantain. There are usually two or three spikes of seeds to each plant.

A good time to gather lesser pond sedge is the summer—it flowers in May or June—whereas the majority of the materials for your palette are collected in the autumn.

It is illustrated overleaf.

VELVET BENT: *Agrostis canina*

Velvet bent is a grass with a loose open head, or panicle, of seeds. These seeds are used individually in picture-making. Each has its own tiny stalk which may well be useful in the picture—so don't trim it off until you are quite certain exactly how you are going to use the seed in your design.

Its stem too can be useful—as can the stems of all the grasses—for birds' legs, perhaps, or water ripples. I used grass stems, for example, to suggest the water in the Crane pictures (Plates 9 and 10, on pages 100–1). If you want to use them in a curve, they must be pinned into position until the glue has set.

Velvet bent grows abundantly in meadows and on moorland.

It is illustrated overleaf.

**LESSER
POND SEDGE**

CAREX ACUTIFORMIS

VELVET BENT
AGROSTIS CANINA

WOOD MILLET: *Milium effusum*

Wood millet is similar to velvet bent, but its seed-head, or panicle, is even looser and more sparse. The grass grows, as its name suggests, in woodland. In colour, the seeds tend to be rather greener than most.

ANNUAL MEADOW GRASS: *Poa annua*
ROUGH MEADOW GRASS: *Poa trivialis*
MEADOW GRASS: *Poa pratensis*

Poa annua, the annual meadow grass, grows abundantly everywhere and flowers almost all the year round. Its floret or seed-head somewhat resembles that of the quaking grasses, but is smaller and more upright and does not quiver. The rough meadow grass, *Poa trivialis*, and meadow grass, *P. pratensis*, are similar, but flower only in the summer.

PAMPAS GRASS: *Cortaderia selloana*

Pampas grass is the enormous grass which, in so many gardens, throws up its whitish silky plumes—sometimes more than ten feet (more than three metres) high. Some nurserymen list more than one variety in their catalogues: it is, for example, possible to get a dwarf variety, and there is also one which has improved, even silkier, plumes.

If the plumes are left on the plant, they will eventually fluff up and the individual seeds will be launched into the air like the seeds of a dandelion clock. I pick the plumes as soon as they are fully out but before they can begin to deteriorate. Unless steps are taken to prevent it, the plumes will continue to "fluff" after picking, so once a plume is dry, I put it into a polythene bag and store it sealed up out of the light. You may even like to try spraying it with hair lacquer to "fix" it.

I have used minute fragments of pampas plumes in miniature work, and pieces in some of my pictures—the breast of the duck in Figure 1, for example—but the grass has been useful to me in work on a much grander scale: the Christmas Crib for St Paul's, illustrated in the plates on pages 109 and 112. There I used complete plumes, spraying them thoroughly but carefully with a matt polyurethane varnish; with a little practice it is possible to spray them so that they retain their original appearance but are completely "fixed", even hard to the touch—if you

49

don't take care, however, a delicate airy plume is transformed into a soggy sticky mess. When I was making more angels for the 1972 Crib, I stripped all the pampas from my friends' gardens, and even had to knock on a complete stranger's door—her garden displayed some splendid clumps, and she generously let me gather some plumes.

BRACKEN: *Pteridium aquilinum*
Bracken is widespread in many areas, and is well-known for the unique golden-brown colour it turns in autumn. The fronds, which are composed of three pinnate sub-sections, are sometimes very large, but where there is plenty of bracken growing it is always possible to find fronds of varying sizes. It is advisable to gather the fronds before they become too dry or they will be brittle and difficult to handle and may well have become curled or twisted. Different-sized individual "pinnae" are very effective arranged in patterns or used, for example, to suggest feathers.

LADY FERN: *Athyrium filix-femina*
Lady fern is one among a number of ferns which are smaller than bracken, and more delicate in shape, but which I use in the same way. Like the male fern (*Dryopteris filix-mas*), it is found in woodland and hedgerows.

Cultivated Flowers—Seeds and Pods
I find a great deal of pleasure in growing and cultivating my own plants: lupin and honesty especially, and the other flowers mentioned here; and globe artichokes too, which I used to decorate the Kings' gifts in the Crib.

HONESTY: *Lunaria annua*, syn. *Lunaria biennis*
Honesty is a popular garden plant which is grown by most people, and certainly by me, because they like its elegant seed-heads. These are shiny silvery-white paper-thin discs, each about an inch across (25 mm), which remain clustered on the stem even after the plant itself has died. They are very attractive, and are, of course, very popular with arrangers of dried flowers.

The silvery disc is, in fact, the inner one of three layers, the two outer ones being coarser in texture and usually a dirty cream colour. The actual seeds are held between the outer "skins" and the pristine inner one—three seeds each side —and are, naturally, flat. They are circular, and are useful in their own right.

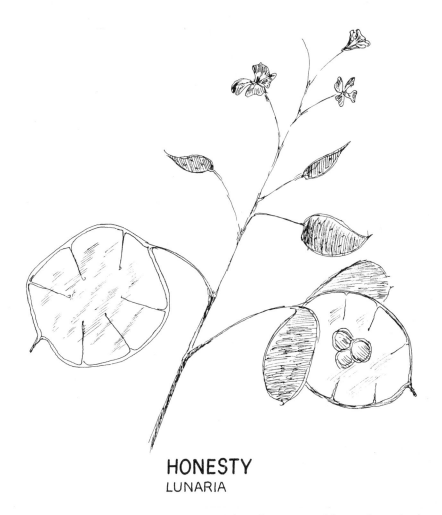

HONESTY
LUNARIA

The coarser outer discs can also be used in picture-making, though the effect is quite different from that of the delicate inner disc.

In the normal course of Nature, the outer skins drop away when the seeds are ripe, releasing them and leaving the silvery inner disc on the plant. I try to gather the seed-heads complete just before the seeds are jettisoned and take the outer discs off carefully myself, so saving the seed (though I often leave them on until just before I am going to use the inner disc, because this helps to protect it —and it needs protection because it is very fragile and cracks or stains all too easily). This can happen from late summer to late autumn, depending on when the plant flowered and what the summer has been like. Store and handle the

51

discs very carefully; splits are almost impossible to repair since even the smallest amount of glue will either show through or stain the delicate skin. The picture called *Bird* 1—Plate 4, on page 77—features the fragile silvery discs.

Honesty seeds should be sown in early autumn and will flower the following April. The flower is mauve, and is made up of clusters of small four-leaved florets. An interesting variety which you may well like to try is "Munstead Purple" which produces purple seed-heads.

ECHINOPS
ECHINOPS RITRO

GLOBE THISTLE: *Echinops ritro* (and other varieties)
Globe thistles are hardy herbaceous plants, some three to four feet high (about a metre) depending on the variety, with deeply incised jagged greyish leaves. The flowers are balls of spiky blue florets which resemble tiny stiff brushes. It is the florets which I use in picture-making—principally for their shape, for the blue colour will fade a little to a steely grey, although it tends to do this less if

52

you gather the flowers promptly, without leaving them on the plant too long. It is thus best to gather the flowers and to dry them, away from the sunlight, as soon as they are fully formed and open.

I have also used globe thistles in three-dimensional work, using the elegant formal heads to adorn the **Kings'** gifts in the Crib.

ORIENTAL POPPY
PAPAVER ORIENTALIS

POPPY: *Papaver*

The annual Shirley (cultivated common) poppy and the biennial Iceland poppy (*Papaver nudicaule*) flower throughout the summer, depending on the time of sowing—the Iceland poppy can indeed be grown as an annual if sown early enough. The oriental poppy (*Papaver orientale*) is a perennial and flowers in June. It is possible to get white, salmon-pink, dark red and orange varieties, as well as the more familiar flaming scarlet.

As far as the seed capsule is concerned, the rule seems to be "The larger and bolder the flower, the larger and stronger and more boldly marked the seed-head." Thus the seed-heads of the Shirley poppy are fragile and delicately marked, while those of the oriental poppy are woody and tough, with raised dark-brown velvety marking on the "cap". I use them for eyes, as I have already mentioned when describing the wild varieties—the Crested Duck in Figure 1 (page 17) is a good example.

The advice about gathering and using the seed-heads of the wild poppies already given on page 29, applies here too—but depending on your garden plans, you may want to be more careful about scattering seed!

LUPIN PODS

LUPIN: *Lupinus*

Lupins, popular herbaceous plants which are not native to Britain, come in many named varieties. Gardeners are usually advised to remove the flower-spike as soon as the flowering is over, to prevent the seed from ripening and to check self-germination; I, however, am at least as interested in the ripe seed as in the flower—and not only in the seed itself, but in the pod too—and face the disapproval of keen gardening friends.

As the lupin florets die, so the familiar seed-pods develop, slightly furry and, at first, a succulent bright green. As the summer progresses the seeds within them ripen until in early autumn the pods are no longer green but dry and brittle and greyish; it is now that they split open along their length to reveal rows of small hard shiny seeds, black or dark brown. I gather the seeds carefully and put them into an envelope, but I leave the open half-pods or shucks still hanging on the stem of the plant, for an extraordinary thing happens to them in mid or late autumn: slowly they begin to twist, turning round and round on themselves until each forms a hollow tube. By this time their colour has darkened and their "fur", though rather threadbare by now, has lost its silky texture and become rough.

These little dark grey tubes, when arranged in rows, remind me strongly of the stylized pictures showing the tightly curled hair and beards of ancient Assyrian kings.

SUNFLOWER: *Helianthus annuus*

The great sunflower plants, some of them six to ten feet tall (from two to three metres) and with flowers as much as a foot across (30 cm), are perhaps the most striking of all the annuals. (If you find them too striking altogether, it is possible to get smaller varieties with several flowers to each plant.) They have usually finished flowering by the end of September, and I then cut the head off and hang it upside down to dry. The petals wither and drop off, followed, with a little help from me, by the dark brown "mat" which formed the centre of the flower. Once this "mat" has gone, the seeds are revealed, in their simple but beautiful and fascinating arrangement. Eventually the individual seeds begin to drop, and I then gather them and throw the rest of the head away. If your garden is a sheltered one, you may be able to leave the flower-head on the plant almost until the seeds are ready to drop; I would in fact advise this, especially if the season is a dry one.

Having gathered the seeds, which are a rather narrow flat heart shape, I store them in a drawer until they are quite dry. They are a silvery grey colour, striped irregularly along their length with cream. The depth of grey varies, as does the distribution of grey and cream: sometimes the seeds are almost all grey, sometimes all cream—no two seeds are exactly the same. As they are rather chunky, I often slit them in half, discarding what is left of the kernel, so that the half-seed can be laid securely flat in the picture.

You can augment your supply of sunflower seeds, and discover a greater colour range including chocolate browns and shiny blacks, if you buy a packet of parrot seed from the pet shop!

SUNFLOWER SEEDS

Vegetable Seeds
I buy vegetable seeds in packets from the seedsman, not to plant but to use in pictures. There are a great many possibilities, of course, but I have found the following three particularly useful—

PARSNIP
Parsnip seeds resemble hogweed seeds, but are smaller and neater. If you have room in the garden, you can, of course, grow a couple of plants, let them run to seed, and so harvest your own seed crop. The body and head of the Hawk—Figure 11, page 99—were created in parsnip seeds.

LETTUCE

Lettuce seeds are small, elongated and straw-coloured. They are useful in miniature work to contrast with darker seeds.

TURNIP

Turnip seeds are quite round, hard little dark brown balls—difficult to handle, but useful when a dark dot is needed, especially for beady pupils in eyes! If you have the patience to do it, they look effective clustered together to resemble Victorian beadwork.

Miscellaneous

There are a number of other bits and pieces which I find useful in my picture-making, the more important of which are listed below. Look along the spice shelf at the grocer's for more ideas—cloves, mixed spice, and chilli peppers (both pod and seed) are some things you may find useful. Things I like to keep by me are—

SPLIT PEAS

Split peas are a rich yellow in colour, circular and dome-shaped; difficult to get hold of with the tweezers, but valuable for their colour and for their waxy texture. The Alphabet—Plate 3, on page 73—is created in split peas and lentils.

LENTILS

Lentils, which are smaller than split peas and a bright orange in colour, are just as useful—and even more difficult to grip!

MELON SEEDS

The black pips of the water melon have two small "eyes" at their tip which give them an odd animal-like character; those of the honeydew melon are similar but creamy-white and eyeless.

Both sorts of melon pips must be washed very thoroughly in cold water before they are stored.

Figure 2 This simple but satisfying star-motif stands in "space", its creamy-brown ash "wings" accentuated by small orange seeds (bought from a seedsman); it was the first picture I ever sold.

PRESERVATION,
PREPARATORY TREATMENTS AND STORAGE

Preserving

In many ways preserving the materials and preparing them for use needs more patience than any other stage in the making of these pictures. So many times I have found a leaf with a new twist or a different shape, and wanted to use it the moment I got it home, only to find myself having to wait until the whole process of pressing it or preserving it in glycerine had been completed.

Most of the seeds and pods which have dried naturally in the sun and wind can be used as soon as you have gathered them, but nearly all the leaves you use will need treatment of one kind or another. Bracken is an exception: you can pick it and use it as soon as it has turned its beautiful golden-brown—although a couple of days under the carpet does help to flatten each piece. Different leaves need to be preserved in different ways. Some are best preserved by pressing, others are happier with the glycerine treatment.

Naturally Dried Materials

There are a number of plants—many of them mentioned in the last chapter—whose seeds, pods and seed-heads need little or no attention, providing you gather them at the right time, when the wind and the sun have done all the necessary preserving for you.

The principal naturally dried leaves, seeds and seed-cases are:

angelica	elm	honesty	parsnip	sunflower
ash	field pennycress	lettuce	plantain	sycamore
caraway	globe thistle	lupin	poppy	thistle
dock	hogweed	monkey puzzle	sorrel	turnip

Once these materials have dried naturally, in the open air, all you have to do is to give the seeds or seed-heads a gentle pull or shake to free them from their stalks. If you are gathering poppies or thistles, cut the heads off with sharp scissors or secateurs. Honesty, because it is so fragile and delicate, needs special attention. Each disc should be cut from the stem separately. I have found that it is better not to peel away the coarser outer "skin" until you actually want to use the silvery inner disc for the skin provides some protection against the disc's cracking across the centre—which, alas, can happen only too easily, and unfortunately repairs are impossible.

A number of grasses can also be collected sun- and wind-dried and ready for use. These are the ones I gather myself:

common wild oat	meadow grass	velvet bent
creeping brown sedge	pampas grass	wood millet
lesser pond sedge	quaking grass	wood small-reed

You will find that you will rarely want to use a complete head of grass, but will instead need to break it up, using individual pieces or even individual seeds. It is, however, best to store the grasses complete, in bunches, and to pick off the individual pieces you want when you are actually at work on your picture. The series of photographs on pages 82-3 illustrates this.

Wood small-reed and pampas grass are best gathered before they become full-blown. When they are fully mature, the heads are fluffy and the seeds, being ripe and ready to leave the parent plant, tend to blow about.

Grass-heads sometimes fluff up *after* they have been gathered, so it is advisable to "fix" them. First make sure that they are absolutely dry; then spray them all over with a fine spray varnish or, for the more delicate specimens, with hair lacquer. Don't overdo it—if you let the spray collect into globules and drips, you'll end up with a sticky soggy mass which will congeal, making it impossible for you to take off the tiny pieces you may need for your pictures.

The Glycerine Treatment

If you want to give leaves the glycerine treatment, you should gather them while they are young and tender, as they will then absorb the glycerine mixture more readily.

Strip the leaves from their branches and lay them in a large dish or bowl. Sprinkle them with a little cooking salt and cover with warm water—warm enough to dissolve the salt. Leave them steeping for twenty-four hours, then pour off the salt water.

Now make up a mixture of glycerine and warm water, using one part glycerine to two parts water, and pour this over the leaves. (You should be able to buy glycerine from any good chemist's or drugstore; it comes "cheaper by the gallon".) Leave them to soak up this mixture for ten days or so—the longer you leave them, the darker they become—and then drain off the liquid and lay the leaves carefully on sheets of newspaper to dry. If you are in a hurry, you can put the leaves between sheets of blotting paper and iron them gently with a warm iron; only do this when it is absolutely necessary, though, for it tends to undo some of the good effect of the glycerine treatment.

Among the leaves which take kindly to the glycerine treatment are the white willow, the crack willow and the ivy; but all the willow family can, I think, be treated in this way, and I am sure there are many others which I have not yet tried myself.

Finding out how different leaves react to different treatments is largely a matter of experiment. Different treatments will often produce different effects in the same leaf, so you may well decide to treat a gathering of, say, gooseberry leaves in two different ways, so that you can achieve and compare two different results.

The glycerine treatment tends to darken a leaf and to make it less brittle— even supple—when dry. Don't, however, rely too much on the effectiveness of a dark glycerined leaf in your picture, for the colour is likely to fade gradually over the years.

Old man's beard, which, like pampas grass, must be cut before it gets too fluffy, can usefully be given a version of the glycerine treatment—as indeed can sprays of willow, beech, oak, and other small tough leaves. In this case you should split the stem of each spray and immerse it first in salt water, then in the glycerine mixture, exactly as before. The glycerine is drawn up the stem into the leaves— or, in the case of old man's beard, the seed-heads—and you can then either hang the whole spray up in your store, or strip off the leaves and seed-heads and store them lying flat. If you decide on the former course, you may have trouble with leaves twisting and curling, so I would advise stripping off some of the leaves, at any rate, and storing them flat, even if you chose to keep some sprays whole and entire. In the case of old man's beard, the glycerine treatment will help to prevent individual "feathers" from drifting away.

Figure 3 An early composition, inspired by one of my first attempts at skeletonizing (described in detail on page 64). I used a Fanny Craddock recipe, which proved excellent, and tried it out on magnolia leaves which, being tough, skeletonize well. The stripped network of veins, in its surgical delicacy, made me think of a fish's backbone; I bleached one slightly, gave it a poppy seed-cap disc backed by silvery honesty for its eye, added fins by cutting another skeletonized leaf along the veins and very gently gluing the pieces to the main leaf, and mounted it on black velvet. I used strands of feathery grass to give an underwater effect.

61

Pressing

Most of us have pressed flowers at some time in our lives, and pressing leaves is no different—it is if anything rather easier, as a leaf is usually stronger than a petal.

Leaves for pressing should be gathered when they are quite dry. Lunch-time on a sunny day is a good time, after the morning dew has gone and before the evening dew forms. Never attempt to collect leaves when they are wet with dew or rain. If the leaves are damp when you press them, they may well become mildewed and have to be thrown away.

Once you have gathered your leaves, look them over carefully for insects, damp, damage and so on. Trim the ends of the stalks. Place the leaves carefully between sheets of clean dry blotting paper, making sure that none of them touch or overlap. Then place the sheets of blotting paper between large books, or between the pages if the books are really big and heavy (telephone directories are very good—*never* use books printed on shiny "art" paper); take care, however, not to fill any one book too full, or the leaves that lie closer to the spine will be more tightly pressed than those at the edges of the page. Pile the books on top of one another to a safe height, and top the pile with a heavy weight. It is important to keep the weight even over the whole surface, so if you don't have a large enough weight put a rigid board on the top book—a chopping board for example—and the weight on top of that.

The leaves should stay in the "press" for as long as possible—certainly not less than six weeks! It is possible to speed up the process by ironing the leaves if you are in a great hurry. Put the leaves between the sheets of clean dry blotting-paper, as usual, and then press them carefully with a warm iron for about five minutes—perhaps a little longer; it depends on the type of leaf being treated. The heat of the iron will make the leaf curl, so you should put it into a pressing book immediately—take care that it is lying flat—and leave it there with a heavy weight on top of it for at least twelve hours. Ironing leaves like this is something of an emergency measure, for it can make them over-brittle and may affect their colour. If you can manage to wait a couple of months, you will get better and safer results.

One small point to remember is that the fleshier the leaf, the longer it will take to press and the likelier it is to lose its colour.

Some leaves definitely prefer to be pressed. These are, in my experience, sea buckthorn, grass-wrack pondweed, yarrow, shrub honeysuckle, yew, raspberry,

62

blackcurrant, and silverweed. Ferns, bracken and blades of grass also appreciate pressing.

Other Preparatory Treatments

There are a number of other treatments which can be used, not to preserve the material but rather to achieve special effects. One of these is skeletonizing, which is adopted when you only want to use the skeleton of the leaf—or just a piece of it, perhaps—for, say, the fins of a fish (Fig. 3 on page 61) or the webbing of a duck's foot. You may, of course, find leaf skeletons lying in ditches during the winter, and with gentle washing in diluted bleach to clean away the dirt, and some gentle pressing, they will be perfectly good to use. But a sure way of always having some by you is to prepare your own.

Bleaching is another treatment, but this is used to achieve a slight variation of shade and, in some cases—ash seed-case "wings", for example—to clean away winter weather stains.

As for dyeing the materials—this is something I have never done. I feel very strongly that the point of these pictures is that they use the *natural* colours of the materials—all the subtle golds, browns, oatmeals and stone colours of the seeds, together with the subtle greens of the leaves. A seed or a pod may sometimes be a bright orange or a deep red, but this is always because it has dried that way naturally—they are *never* artificially coloured. Once you begin colouring your materials by artificial means, you are employing quite different techniques to achieve quite different effects: it is an altogether different affair.

Skeletonizing

Skeletonizing is not a treatment designed to preserve material but a treatment to get a special effect, and as such is more akin to bleaching than to glycerining or pressing. Leaf skeletons are quite extraordinarily fascinating and delicate things, and have, for me, the same sort of appeal as snowflakes photographed under a microscope.

The commonest use for leaf skeletons is, I suppose, to make Christmas table decorations, but I have also found it useful to have some of them to hand for use in my pictures. As I have said earlier, you *may* come across leaf skeletons in ditches or on a pile of old leaves raked up and left to rot months earlier, but although some are perfectly usable, others are broken or much too dirty, so it is often more satisfactory, and really quite simple, to prepare your own.

This is the best skeletonizing recipe I have come across. It looks rather daunting, but is really very easy once you get going. One word of warning: keep small children and household pets firmly away, and do wear rubber gloves for the ingredients are rather strong.

Dissolve three ounces (80 grammes, or three tablespoons) of washing soda in two pints (one litre, or five cupfuls) of boiling water, then add an ounce and a half (40 grammes, or one and a half tablespoons) of slaked quick-lime. Boil for ten minutes in a very old has-been saucepan. Strain carefully; wash out the saucepan; tip the mixture back in and re-boil. Now add the leaves and boil fast for an hour, adding more water as necessary to replace that lost by evaporation. To test if the leaves are ready, fish one out, rinse it carefully under cold water and rub it gently between the fingers. If its skin comes away easily the leaf is ready; if not, continue boiling, checking at intervals, until it does. Then fish the leaves out carefully one by one, rub each gently, and rinse away all traces of the "flesh".

If necessary, you can then bleach the skeletons. Do not, however, leave them in the bleach longer than is absolutely necessary or they will become very brittle, cracking and fracturing at the slightest pressure. After bleaching, rinse them thoroughly in cold water and lay them on newspaper to drain. Before they are quite dry, press them.

Bleaching

Bleaching leaves and seeds is a very simple process. The only two important things you must remember are, first, keep small children and any household pets well out of the way, and secondly, always wear a pair of rubber gloves.

Plate 1 This turkey was inspired by a picture in a part-work which my young son was collecting. The sketch came nice and quickly – sometimes, however, I struggle over and over to get an idea into shape, and occasionally have been forced to abandon one altogether because the sketch just wouldn't come right. I can't really draw at all, and my husband has often rescued me, pointing out that the reason a sketch feels wrong is because, anatomically speaking, I have drawn a wing- or shoulder-joint that simply wouldn't work. The turkey's body is silverweed and grass, his wings are glycerined willow leaves tipped with bleached aspidistra, and his eye and claws are dried African seeds.

I use ordinary domestic bleach for cleaning and bleaching. It is difficult to give exact quantities since the amount I use depends on how white I want the materials; it really is a matter of trial and error!

However, when I simply want to *clean* seeds—ash seeds, for instance—that have become weather-worn during the winter months, I usually find that a solution of one-third bleach to two-thirds water is about right. Put the seeds into a large *plastic or china* bowl and cover them with the bleach solution (they should be well-covered). In about half an hour to an hour, the seeds should be nice and clean—*not* necessarily lighter in shade, but with the weather stains cleaned away. Now put them in a colander or sieve, and rinse them *thoroughly*. This is vitally important—if you don't remove *all* the bleach solution, the seeds will begin to rot. Then spread them out on sheets of newspaper to dry—preferably in a sunny window, *not* on top of the cooker or in front of the fire. If you try to hurry up the drying process by putting your seeds in the oven or on the hearth rug, they will begin to curl and will lose their natural shape; this applies to *all* seeds.

If you want actually to *bleach* leaves and seeds, rather than simply clean them, you should step up the quantity of bleach so that your solution is made up of equal parts of bleach and water—or even stronger if the leaves are still green. You can leave them soaking for two to three hours, giving them a stir with a wooden spoon every now and then (I keep a spoon for this especial purpose). As soon as you have achieved the shade you want, quickly rinse the leaves or seeds and spread them out to dry. Seeds can be left to dry on newspaper, as described in the last paragraph, but with leaves I have found it best to shake off the excess solution and then put them between sheets of clean dry blotting paper and press them dry, or they lose their shape badly.

The best thing to do is to experiment for yourself, both with the amount of bleach you use and the time you leave your seeds and leaves to soak. You will find you can get some very subtle shades and effects with different materials. But whatever else you do, *don't forget to rinse*, or all your careful work and patient experimenting will go for nothing.

Storage
Whether your materials are sun- or wind-dried, glycerined, pressed, skeletonized or bleached, they must all be labelled and stored in such a way that you can get

at what you want quickly and easily. A date on the label is also useful.

Storing seeds presents little problem. I have a number of boxes which vary in size from match-box to shoe-box, and these hold most of the seeds I collect. For some very tiny seeds I use envelopes. I label each box or envelope carefully with the name of the seed, the date on which it was stored, and a short note about any peculiarity of shape or colour. Seeds and seed-carriers differ surprisingly according to where the parent plant has grown, how much sun there was, how much rain, and so on, so this is important.

I am fortunate in that I found and bought an old dentistry cabinet, dating from the Victorian period, which has two columns of shallow drawers, originally designed to hold a grisly collection of scrapers, drill bits and other tools for poking and pushing. In this I keep my stock of the seeds I use most frequently. It is also possible to buy small sets of drawers about eighteen inches (about fifteen centimetres) high—half a dozen drawers to a chest—in the Whitewood section of large department stores, and these are compact and tidy. However, chests of this kind are something of a luxury, and all you really need is a collection of differently sized boxes. Seal up any gaps at the corners of your boxes with sticky brown paper strip.

You can also use polythene bags for storage, and these have one great advantage in that you can see at once what is inside them, thus saving you from making descriptive notes (though you should still write a label with the date of storage on it); if you use them for leaves, though, you must make sure that the leaves lie flat; and you must always take care that no moisture is trapped inside the bag or its contents, whether leaves or seeds, will mildew.

One way of making sure that pressed or glycerined leaves stay flat is to put them, still between their sheets of blotting paper, under the spare room carpet. Don't, however, put them under a carpet which is constantly being walked on or regularly hoovered, as the leaves may well get broken and split.

Mark each sheet of blotting paper clearly so that you won't have to hunt through your stock, disturbing it unnecessarily and risking damaging it, in order to find, say, the willow leaf you need for one particular picture.

A neater and more convenient method of storing prepared leaves is to place them, still in their sheets of blotting paper, one on top of the other on a flat surface, inserting at intervals a sheet of hardboard which is slightly larger than the sandwiches of blotting paper. Stick a label on each layer of blotting paper, so that it pokes out from the edge of the pile like the tabs one sees in alphabetical files or the section tabs in books of paper patterns, and can be easily read. (The hardboard sheets are very useful: they enable you to lift off a whole block of layers smoothly and easily if you need to get at a leaf which you have stored—as one always seems to do—at the bottom of the pile.)

If you have collected a large quantity of one particular kind of leaf, you can dispense with the blotting paper sandwich idea, and instead fill an entire book with, say, silverweed leaves, placing them directly between the pages. Telephone directories come into their own here, but if you are using them, or any other book printed on very thin paper, for this kind of storage, be sure to leave a dozen or so pages between each spread of leaves, or you may find that the stalk or skeleton of one leaf will "print through" onto another.

When you are storing or pressing leaves, never use books printed on a shiny coated "art" paper—at the slightest suggestion of moisture the leaves will stick fast to the pages and tear when you try to get them off again.

Transparent boxes are naturally very convenient for storing, but they, like polythene bags, have a tendency to collect moisture, especially if left in the sun.

All materials, indeed, are best stored well out of the sun—ideally in a dry cool dark place.

Grasses and sprays of glycerined leaves should be hung upside down until they are quite dry, and then stored flat in a drawer between sheets of newspaper.

A final word of warning: most of these materials are very attractive to mice. I speak from bitter experience as I have had drawersful of the most beautiful materials destroyed by mice in the course of what cannot have been more than two or three weeks.

The ideal situation to be in, of course, is to have a room set aside as a work-room or studio, in which you can prepare and store your materials, and work on

Plate 2 The peacock's neck is of hogweed, his body ash "wings" and wild oats, his tail bleached aspidistra leaves interspersed with long grass stalks which are tipped with more wild oats. His feet shame me, since I was unable to find anything that was the right shape, as well as being the right texture and colour, so I compromised and cut some out of leaves; I have frequently split leaves along their natural veins, but never before snipped out a shape with scissors, and wish now that I'd stuck, as always before and since, to naturally-formed material. This design, deliberately stylized, was inspired by a motif on a carrier bag which happened to catch my eye.

Figure 4 The greenhouse which we decided to use as my store and workroom. The black-out is to prevent an excess of light and heat; it hasn't, however, been so easy to exclude the mice from the neighbouring cornfield. On the table lie a telephone book full of dried and pressed hedgerow maple leaves, and some oriental seed-heads.

creating your pictures. Such a room would ideally be furnished with several old chests of drawers (really deep drawers), many wide shelves, and a long work-table; there would be good daylight; a variety of lamps and overhead lighting would be available; and in addition, a power point for an electric kettle, an easy chair—and *no* telephone.

However, successful storage of your materials is largely a matter of common sense. Keep them dry, keep them flat, keep them carefully labelled and easily accessible—and keep them safe from mice!

EQUIPMENT

ONCE YOU HAVE collected your materials and prepared them ready for use, you will probably be impatient to begin work on your first picture! All the time that you have been collecting and pressing and bleaching and skeletonizing, you have been thinking of the different ways you could use each seed or leaf, and now at last the moment has come—or *almost* come, for you will need one thing more before you can get started: the tools of your trade.

What do you need to gather round you in the way of equipment? There is no mystery about this. You will find that in fact you need very little, none of it costing much.

The choice of "tools" does depend on the size of the materials you are working with. If, for example, you are using fairly large leaves, you can pick them up with your fingers—but you won't find it so easy to manage when it comes to grass seeds or poppy seeds. For these you will need tweezers. Ideally you should provide yourself with several different pairs with varying styles of grip, to pick up and hold the different seeds and leaves *without damaging them.*

A scalpel, too, is very useful if you want to pare a seed slightly to modify its shape or to slice a piece of leaf to achieve some special effect. This *can* be done with sharp nail scissors, but a scalpel is more precise and you really do need precision tools for this precision work.

Plate 3 This alphabet, created from split peas and lentils and mounted on brown hopsack, was inspired by a Victorian sampler. I drew the letters freehand with chalk, but they seemed to get bigger as I worked; I was just thinking, with some surprise, that it fitted nicely, when I found I had forgotten Z and had to tuck it at the bottom.

72

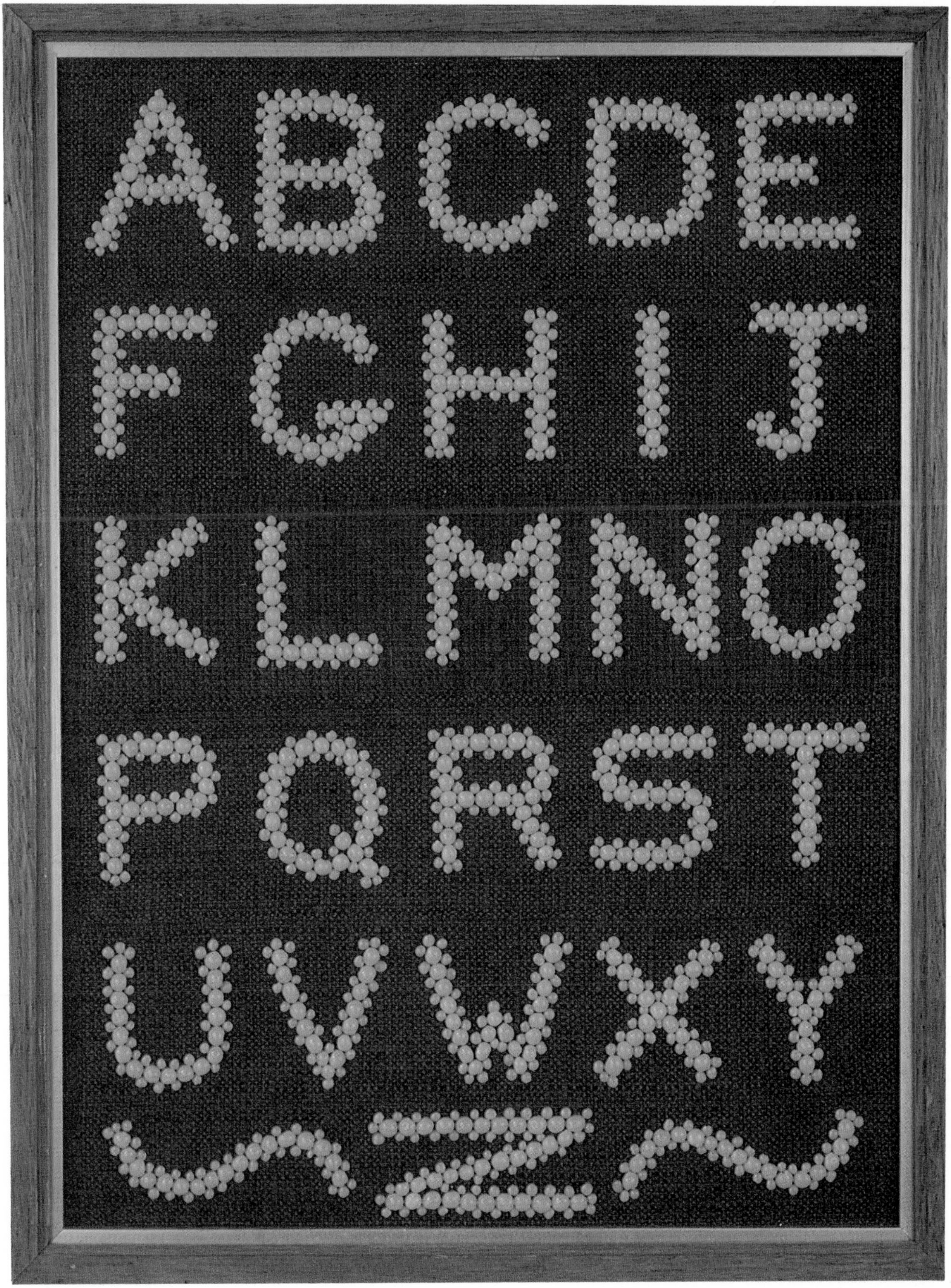
ABCDE
FGHIJ
KLMNO
PQRST
UVWXY
Z

I was lucky and was given a surgical scalpel, but at most good stationery shops you can buy what they call a "trimming knife" which works just as well; buy a set of spare blades at the same time, so that you can replace each one as soon as it becomes blunt.

To stick the seeds and leaves into place, you will need adhesive. Copydex is by far the best I have come across, and, most important, the most *manageable*. All the other solutions I have tried have proved to be either not sticky enough, or too sticky to handle. Copydex has an added advantage: it goes transparent when dry. Use the tube, which is a little more expensive, rather than the pot and brush, or you will find you get through so much that you have to keep on buying fresh supplies. The tube is also easier to control, I think—one needs only the slightest amount of Copydex on each seed. If you cannot get Copydex, however, experiment with other brands.

You will also need some cotton sheeting for the base of your picture. Old pillowcases and sheets are ideal for this. Not only can you draw on the sheeting when stretched—I go into more detail about this in Chapter 4—but it absorbs Copydex very well. Thin paper, of airmail quality, is very useful if you want to make a miniature using, say, grass seeds and poppy seeds, for it does not "give" and if you want to cut round it when the work is finished, you can do so easily.

All you need now is a soft pencil (2B or 3B) and a felt pen, and you are ready to begin—at last!

As you go along you will probably find other "tools" that you can't do without—but this is very much a matter of personal choice. I find, for example, that I am lost without a darning needle with which to "stroke" Copydex onto the finer grass seeds, and an old toothbrush with which to clean the fabric that I use for mounting. Remember, *there are no rules;* I can only talk about the equipment I have found best when making my pictures. You may find and use quite different tools—anything at all—knitting needles, razor blades—*anything* at all that you are happy handling and working with.

MAKING A PICTURE

THERE IS NO limit at all to the sort of design or picture you can make with these materials—portraits,   abstract designs, miniatures, anything you choose. What one has to remember, of course, is that one is dealing with materials which have an intrinsic interest: one should try to display the "raw materials" so that their shape and subtle colour are shown to the best advantage, in such a way that the final result will be more intriguing and interesting.

There are many ways of setting about making a picture with natural materials, and I am sure that everyone who tries it will develop a method of his own, and that it may well be quite different from mine. The only "right way" is the way that is "right" for you, and the only criterion of success is that it works—for you. This is the way that works for me.

I begin by sketching my design or picture, sometimes in considerable detail with shading, on to a rough sheet of paper. Sometimes the picture is right the first time. Sometimes I experiment several times before I am satisfied. Occasionally I cannot get down on paper what I have in mind at all, and in that case I have to abandon the idea, at least for the time being. Eventually, however, I have a finished sketch on the paper in front of me, exactly the same size as the finished picture will be. Figure 6 on page 79 shows one of these sketches, ready to be transferred to the backing fabric on which the actual picture will be composed. Before the sketch is transferred to the fabric, I usually have a clear idea of the materials I will use to "realize" the picture. Often the materials themselves will have suggested the picture.

I then take a softer blacker pencil or a felt pen and trace over the outline of my sketch, clarifying and simplifying as much as possible, and I generally outline the main areas of highlight and shadow at the same time, where this is going to be helpful.

I have now to transfer my simplified line drawing to a piece of stretched cotton or linen. There are two possible ways of doing this. You can either use carbon paper—laying the carbon paper face down on the stretched fabric, and the sketch face up on top of it, and then tracing fairly lightly over the sketch, just hard enough to leave a clear impression on the fabric—or you can make the outline sketch so black that you can lay the stretched fabric over it and still see the outline beneath, thus enabling you to copy it onto the fabric. If you are *very* confident, you may decide to skip the outline-sketch-on-paper stage and draw your idea direct onto the fabric; however, this can be risky, since you want to keep the fabric as clean as possible, and any attempts to change or correct a line may dirty it very quickly.

Before you can transfer your sketch, however, the fabric must be stretched taut. You may like to use an embroidery frame for doing this—at least for small pictures—but I much prefer to stick the cotton onto a piece of cardboard; in which case, of course, it is on this cardboard that I draw my initial sketch, which will then show through the stretched cotton.

I smear a small amount of adhesive round the edge of the cardboard and then lay the cotton or linen, pulled taut, onto it. Make sure that the vertical/ horizontal weave of the fabric is not pulled out of shape, as if it is, it may cause distortion later. Whichever method of transferring your design to your fabric you choose to adopt, or if you decide to draw straight onto the fabric, it is easier to stretch the cotton onto the cardboard *first*. Make sure that it is stuck down all round the edge. It helps if you iron it first and make absolutely sure there are no wrinkles or creases.

Now at last you are ready to begin. The outline of your design is there, sketched on the taut fabric; your tweezers, your adhesive and your other "tools" lie ready; and of course, your collection of seeds, leaves and assorted materials is to hand. Fig. 6 on page 79 shows my own equipment assembled

Plate 4 The whole craft really began here, for this is the first picture I ever made. I had been experimenting with glycerining some willow leaves, and had spread them out to dry when I noticed how lively and flourishing they looked, like a bird's tail-feathers. There happened to be some honesty in the house, so using that and the leaves I tried out various ideas until this came – *Bird 1*. I found the frame later, in a junk-yard; nowadays I often take an unusual frame – round or oval or carved – and design a picture to fit it, but in this first instance the discovery of a suitable frame was as happily impromptu as that of the design. I couldn't bear to sell this picture, although we have had offers for it over and over, so I gave it to my husband, who has it still.

Figure 5 I was wandering around the Fitzwilliam Museum in Cambridge when I saw a ring which had, framed in the bezel, a miniature wheatsheaf; as soon as I got home I started work on my first miniature, and now enjoy making them more, if possible, than the larger pictures. This one (which is in reality slightly smaller than shown here) is created from tiny cream-coloured seeds on a background of coffee-coloured Jap silk, mounted in a Victorian locket-frame of the kind many jewellers have in stock. This one is double-sided, and I made a design incorporating the initials of the owner which were engraved on the reverse. Such lockets, often designed to take a lock of hair, are ideal for miniatures.

ready, together with the sketch. But before you even pick up a seed with the tweezers, you must have a fairly clear idea of the overall effect you are trying to create: you must know, that is, to which part of the seed you are going to apply the adhesive, which part will be fastened flat against the fabric, which part will be slightly raised above the surface. This principle holds true for all materials, but is perhaps most easily demonstrated by considering the ways in which one can use an ash seed—or rather, the "wing" which carries the seed.

If you pick up the wing by the thick end (which contains the seed) and apply adhesive to the flatter end, you will find that your picture has a much rougher texture than if you reverse the process. Some of these ash wings also have a pronounced twist, and accordingly the angle at which they are placed on the fabric backing has its own effect on the look and texture of the picture. If you decide to trim off the thicker end of the wing, you can get it to sit much flatter on the fabric. You can even choose a wing which has little or no twist, trim the ends flat, apply adhesive over at least two-thirds of its under-surface, and set it in place so that it lies quite flat, creating still another effect.

Because of the irregular shape of the materials with which you are working, it is necessary to overlap the seeds if the backing fabric is not to show through between them. The way in which this overlapping is achieved depends very

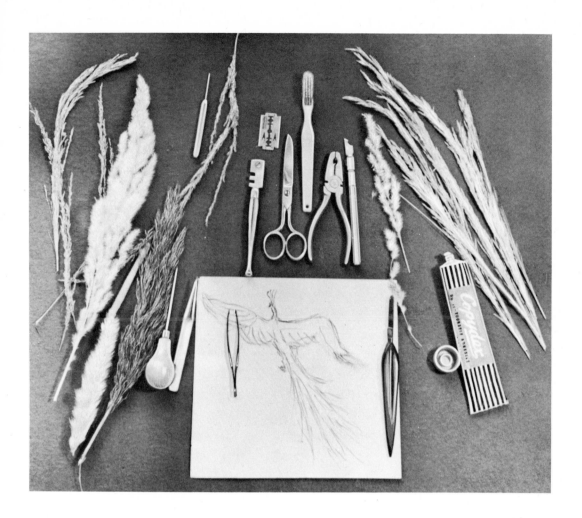

Figure 6 My equipment assembled ready for work. Around the sketch, waiting to be transferred to the fabric backing, lie (left to right): dried grasses and reeds; two bradawl-type tools for making screw-holes in the frame (it is important to fix the picture-wire, etc., *before* one slips the picture into its frame, or vibration may shake seeds loose), tweezers (for picking up seeds), glass-cutters, a razor blade (for cutting misplaced seeds free from adhesive), scissors, a toothbrush (if any specks of dust fall on the mounting fabric I carefully brush them off it with this), pliers (for extracting nails, etc., from old frames), a scalpel, Copydex, another scalpel.

79

much on the personal preference of the artist. I like to work from the bottom upwards, laying each fresh seed on top of the previous one, so that they overlap like tiles on a roof. You may, however, prefer to lift the first seed, which is already fixed at one edge, and slip the second seed under it. If you follow this method, it is advisable to put *a very little* adhesive on the upper surface of the seed, smearing the part that is to be slid under the seed already in position, as well as putting the usual smear on the underside to stick the seed to the backing fabric. The series of photographs on pages 82–3 (Figure 7) may help here.

When you are applying the adhesive be careful not to use too much. I find that usually the best way is to squeeze a blob of Copydex onto a saucer; then, before the adhesive starts to dry and its surface to skin over, I take my seed in the tweezers, holding it carefully so that the section I want to stick onto the fabric is properly positioned, and stroke it gently against the blob.

If you do make a mistake, and want to lift off a seed once you have stuck it into place, take a firm hold of it with the tweezers and pull gently. You may, however, find that the dry rubbery Copydex begins to pull away too, dragging with it a number of other seeds or dislodging them from their positions, so be prepared to cut out the awkward seed with sharp nail scissors if necessary. It is not too difficult when you are dealing with hard shiny seeds, but it can be very tricky if you are working with the furrier sort of grass seed. The problem is aggravated if you are using paper as your backing material instead of fabric, since whereas Copydex generally sinks into fabric and grips each seed individually, on paper it tends to stick to itself and form a continuous rubber mat— pull one seed, and twenty or thirty may come away at one go!

I have found that when I am working on a miniature, of the kind shown in Figure 5 on page 78—anything, perhaps, less than three inches (75 mm) square— and using the tiniest seeds, cotton is too floppy and loosely textured to be a suitable backing material, and I prefer to work on a thin good quality paper, or even on good quality tracing paper.

Whatever backing material you use, once the picture is completed you simply cut round the design (Chapter 5 describes this), carefully trimming away all evidence of the paper or fabric backing; looked at from the front, it will not be seen once the frame is in place; yet it provides a strong and flexible backing to hold seeds and leaves in position.

It often happens that not all parts of the design can be executed on the same piece of backing. When I made the pair of Crane pictures shown on pages 100–1,

Plate 5 A good many of my pictures are of birds, and I wanted to try something different, something more heraldic, so I worked out this St. George design. The saint's body is mailed in hogweed seeds, picked *before* they ripened when they still had a greenish tinge (this was three years ago; I shall be interested to see whether they fade in time), his spear a stalk of grass, his horse ash wings maned with grass, his dragon – suitably – thistle.

81

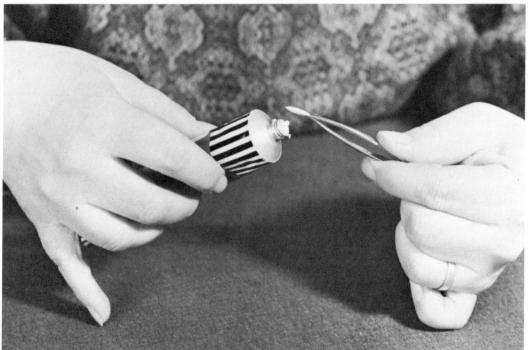

Figure 7 a, b and c   This series of photographs shows how a single seed is selected and slipped into place. Before I even detach the seed from its stem, I consider exactly how it will fit into my picture: in which direction must it "flow"? to which part of it will I apply the glue? which surface will stand proud of the mounting or backing material? When I am perfectly sure what I mean to do, I grip the appropriate part of the seed gently but firmly in the tweezers – here, as it happens, I was using pampas grass which had been delicately sprayed with fixative. I then stroke the seed gently against a blob of glue – it is important not to use too much; sometimes, as here, I squeeze it direct from the tube, at other times I squeeze some out onto a saucer. And lastly I tuck it into place. It looks finicky, but is really quite easy.

for example, I built up the head, neck, wings and body just as I have described, on a piece of cotton. I wanted to make the legs from some carefully selected pieces of cornstalk with a joint closely resembling the bird's leg-joint (the one that looks like a human knee bending the wrong way). It was obviously impracticable to mount the fragile legs on the cotton, since it would have been impossible to cut the backing material away afterwards, so, having chosen the cornstalk legs and the tiny leaf tip claws, I later assembled the picture directly onto its final background of black velvet. The mounting process is described in more detail in Chapter 5.

As I mentioned earlier, there is no real limit to the type of design that can be made with these natural materials, and there is also no limit to the number of ways in which one can execute that design. You can, for example, create flat unshaded areas outlined in darker seeds, as one would use a dark outline in a line drawing. You can, on the other hand, deliberately vary the colour and tone of each seed, building up mass and form in a manner akin to shading. The great thing to remember is that the materials have their own form and their own vitality, which must be recognized and used to the best advantage.

Directional application is important here: you must set the seed in place so that it is pointing in the right direction, suggesting the form and the flow of line you want to achieve. This is perhaps shown most clearly in the portrait head, created chiefly from hogweed seeds, which is shown opposite and overleaf, with a detailed sketch to illustrate the directional flow. The hogweed seeds were laid on in curves and swirls to bring out the moulding of the forehead and of the cheekbones. Similarly, in the picture of St George and the Dragon, shown in Plate 5, the ash "wings" used to create the horse's legs were laid on in line with the direction of the legs themselves. This method of directional application can be very clearly seen in mosaic work with leaves and seeds.

Finally, a word of warning about honesty: its silvery disc has to be handled especially carefully. Not only is it particularly fragile and all too ready to crack across the middle, but it is also, of course, translucent, and tends to become more so with age. This means that the backing material must be absolutely clean and smooth, and that you must be very careful to apply your smear of Copydex *only* at the very edges of the disc, and then as sparingly as possible.

Exactly how you use your materials will naturally depend on your vision and

Plate 6   Portrait of a man (described above and overleaf).

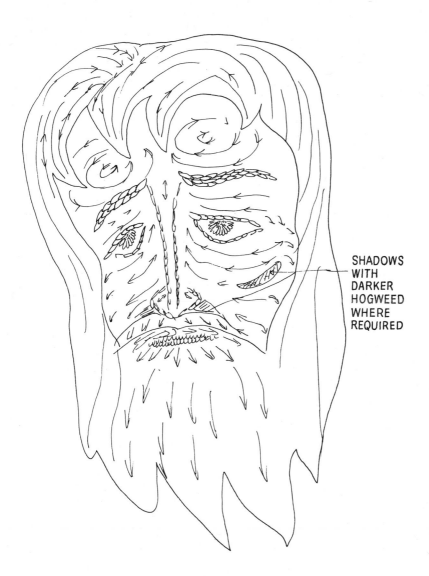

SHADOWS
WITH
DARKER
HOGWEED
WHERE
REQUIRED

Figure 8   This was the first portrait I ever tried to create in seeds, and was taken from the life – my sitter was extremely patient. It is shown in colour overleaf, but I have also added an ordinary photograph and a diagram so that you can see the technique in rather more detail. The hair, beard and eyebrows were carried out in ash seeds, extracted from the winged seed-cases which I use so often in other work; the flesh in hogweed; and the pupils and irises of the eyes in the petals of everlasting flowers. When I drew the sketch for the portrait, I planned the highlights very carefully and tried to vary the shades of material I used to give the effect of flesh tints, moulding over cheek-bones, and so on. The outline drawing above shows the directional "flow" of the seeds in a similar portrait.

87

your skill. Control of texture, and its subtle variation, and the ability to create form and to suggest mass are skills possessed by the artist in most of the different ways of making pictures, not just in this particular field. The only advice I feel I can really give is the age-old "Look and see". Examine the seeds and leaves you have collected; play with them, turning them round and round on a sheet of paper; and see what their colour and their form suggest to you.

Plate 7 The idea for this design actually came to me as I was sitting in the dentist's waiting room, taking my mind off the session to come by looking through his copies of the *National Geographic Magazine*. In one issue there was an article about some religious festival in South America, and photographs of a splendid procession. The crucifers carried crosses of many different shapes, most of them decorated with religious scenes – I wasn't that ambitious, but I liked the idea of creating a small portrait cross. It was almost my first attempt at a small composition, its only predecessor being a copy I made of Christ's head from the Syon Cope in the Victoria and Albert Museum, using my seeds as the Syon embroiderers had used their stitches rather than as tesserae in a mosaic. I used shrub honeysuckle leaves for the cross, getting in as much variation of colour as possible to accentuate their strange snakeskin quality. Christ's hair and beard are of reed, his eyebrows of seeds taken from within the reeds, and the iris and pupil of each eye is made of clustered poppy seeds. He is haloed in translucent silvery honesty.

MOUNTING AND FRAMING

THE FIRST STEP in framing your work is determined by whether you have made a picture or design which fills the entire frame so that none of the fabric or other backing material is seen, or whether you have designed something which is meant to stand in space surrounded by a neutral "mounting" material, like the Gryphon on the facing page.

If your picture is of the "all-over" kind, you will probably have already chosen its frame, or will, at least, have the exact size in mind. Take the frame and measure the back of it. You must now cut a piece of stiff card which will fit into the frame, carefully allowing for the fact that the edge of the backing material, on which you have assembled your picture, must be folded over the edge of the card, so that it will be gripped firmly between the card and the frame and will not move once placed in position.

Now take your picture on its fabric or paper backing. Lay it face down on the table. Place the piece of card over it. Check to make sure that the picture is correctly centred and all-square on the piece of card, and then fold the edges of the backing material over the back of the card, all the way round, and stick them down with Copydex—used sparingly!

Figure 9 This particular picture was inspired by its dark elaborate frame. I felt this needed a heraldic design and decided on a gryphon – I wanted a formal severe creature, since the frame itself was already quite romantic enough. His body is created from ash "wings", his eyebrow and beak and the tip of his tail from sunflower seeds, and his tail from parsnip seeds reversed. On this occasion, I abandoned my favourite mounting fabrics – the "disappearing" black velvet and the brown hopsack which sets off creamy and golden shades – and mounted him on rich deep wine-coloured velvet.

On the other hand, if your picture is so designed that it should stand in space against a neutral "mounting", your first step is choosing the mounting material. Here again, personal taste is the deciding factor. Almost any material will do, from fine silk to wood veneers. I have two favourite materials—black velvet and dark brown hopsack; and of these two, the one I have used most is the black velvet. There is one very good reason for this: it disappears. Yes, exactly that! When it is clean and flat behind the glass of the frame, you simply cannot see it is there. Consequently a picture mounted on black velvet has every possible opportunity of showing itself off to its best advantage, and the subtle colours and shapes of the seeds and leaves are easier to appreciate because of the lack of competition from the surrounding material. I use brown hopsack when, for one reason or another, a black velvet mount seems to provide too strong a contrast, or to make too over-stated an effect, for the particular picture in question.

Sometimes, of course, the mounting material will positively enhance a picture. On the facing page is a picture (Plate 8) which I made showing a small reed-warbler balancing on a slender reed stem. I mounted this, as you can see, on a piece of dark green water-silk. The colour of the silk echoed the greenish tint in the materials I had used, and the watered effect in the weave of the fabric seemed very satisfactorily to suggest something of the watery habitat of the bird. The overall effect seems to me somehow intriguingly Chinese.

That piece of silk was an odd scrap from a rag-bag, which illustrates another maxim: "Never throw any odd piece of fabric away!" It is worthwhile hanging

Plate 8   This picture of the reed-warbler is an example of a design created to suit one specific frame. Some friends showed me this antique Strasbourg frame, an heirloom which had been handed down for generations, and asked me to make a picture to fit it. I decided what sort of shape I would need – something small and elegant, like the frame itself, but fairly simple to balance its elaborate curlicues – and flipped through my son's *Birds of the World* until I found something suitable. The warbler's back is made of a kind of dried Spanish seed which has a lustrous quality, his tail of split bleached aspidistra, his beak of sunflower seeds. (The body of the Egyptian bird in Figure 13 on page 107 is composed of the same sort of Spanish seeds as are here used for the warbler's back.) This picture is an example of the way in which one can build up a composition in parts: the head and body of the bird were composed on a piece of cotton backing and were then glued into place, as a single unit, on the silk mounting material; I then added the tail feathers, legs, feet and reed-stem, gluing them directly and oh! *so* carefully onto the silk.

on to any odd pieces of interesting fabric that come your way—you never know when they may come in useful. An old dress at a rummage sale, one you could not possibly wear, might very well provide just the right piece of odd material to back a new picture. The muted colours of old and faded fabrics are frequently more satisfactory for mounting purposes than the clearer colour of new materials.

The mounting fabric must, of course, be clean and smooth—and here I must add a word of warning about black velvet which, though excellent as a mounting material, does show every tiny speck of dust and dirt. When you are using it, you must keep the working area as clean and dust-free as possible. I keep several damp tooth-brushes handy, and use them to lift any speck off the velvet the moment I notice it.

Once you have chosen your mounting material, cut the piece of stiff card or board to fit the back of the picture, as described on page 90, and fasten the mounting material over it, exactly as before—though in this case, of course, you are spared the worry of trying to align the picture correctly; be careful to check that the grain/weave of the fabric runs parallel with the picture frame, or the final effect will be disconcertingly lopsided. Now place your design on the mounting material, positioning it carefully, and when you are perfectly certain that you have it right, stick it down with a little Copydex. Use as little adhesive as possible, and be very very careful. A false step at this stage, a smear of Copydex in the wrong place, and you may have to start all over again with a fresh piece of mounting material! It should be fairly straightforward if your design is a single all-of-a-piece composition complete on one piece of backing material; the fun comes when you have to assemble more than one piece on your mount. Work out before-hand just where you are going to put your adhesive—as little

Figure 10 When I had made the picture of the dragon worried by flies which is used on the jacket of this book, I thought I would use the idea again featuring a large bird. Up until this time all the birds I had made had been, I think, essentially decorative. This one, however, very soon showed his aggressive, angry personality – and became none the less a favourite because of that! The body is composed of hogweed, bristled with thistle spikes. The wings are made from bleached ash "wings" and are tipped with bleached split sections of aspidistra leaves. The tail is also aspidistra, and the beak is made from a piece of trimmed monkey puzzle spike. The crest is made from a piece of wild oat, and the eye, a black seed surrounded by a bright orange fleshy rim, comes from an African seed-head found in a dried flower shop. The "flies" are wild oats with heads of parsnip seeds and eyes of small lupin seeds.

94

as possible, in as few places as possible—so that the final positioning can be sure and deliberate. To remove Copydex from any material is difficult enough, and to get it off black velvet without leaving an ugly mark is almost impossible, as I have sadly discovered.

If you do happen to spill a small drop of Copydex onto the fabric, don't smear it by trying to remove it when it is still wet. Let it dry, and then try to lift it carefully but steadily off. If you are lucky, the rubbery elastic blob of adhesive will pull away from the fabric with no damage. It cannot and will not do this, however, if it has soaked in at all.

Once you have your picture securely on its mounting, and firmly stuck to its backing board, you must turn your attention to the framing. The easiest way to get your work framed is to take it along to a professional framer, choose the style of frame you like, tell him how you want it to look, and leave the rest to him. I go to a professional framer when I want a modern frame, or a particularly un-usual frame which has to be specially made, but usually I frame my pictures myself. I am particularly fond of old plain wood frames, not necessarily antiques, because I believe that the sort of picture I make looks best in them. A new gold-coloured frame, for example, looks somehow too brash and strident, and lacks the quietly enhancing effect of old plain wood.

I am always on the look-out for odd frames in antique shops and junk shops, and have found some quite extraordinary ones—square, round, oval, carved. Naturally such frames have to be matched very carefully to their picture—more often than not, an unusual frame will actually suggest a picture to suit its style. This was, for example, the case with the Reed-warbler (Plate 8, page 93) and the Gryphon (Figure 9, page 91). I particularly enjoy designing pictures to fit into round and oval frames. The important thing to remember is that in the final effect, picture and frame should form a single unit, so that "the whole is greater than the sum of the parts".

When looking for frames, I have learned, by trial and error, to be very dis-criminating! At first I would eagerly buy up any frame which caught my eye, only to be disappointed later when, in spite of much careful cleaning and refurbishing, it was still not quite good enough to be on display. Nowadays when a frame attracts my attention, I check carefully to see that it is not warped, cracked or split (especially at the corners) and that the joints fit snugly. If a joint has been cut accurately in the first place, and has not warped or twisted out of shape, a loose joint can easily be fixed with a modern wood glue. It is also important to watch out for woodworm and wormholes!

If the frame has a gilded "slip" between the glass and the outer frame, I make sure that this is intact and that its gold leaf skin is not badly worn or patchy—it is extremely difficult to match the original gold leaf with a modern gold paint. You may, of course, buy a new "slip" and have this fitted if you wish, but old ones very often have a silvery gleam which modern ones sadly lack. The best new gilding product I have yet discovered is called Goldfinger; this is a paste which you rub on with your finger, allow to dry, and then polish. It has a good soft colour, which is neither too metallic and coppery nor too bright and yellow. With this, as with all products, it is important to follow the maker's instructions and to check whether it must be kept away from children and pets.

If the frame has its original glass in it, check that this is not too badly scratched —the slightest graze will show up in front of black velvet—and that it has no bad bubbles or distortions. The older the glass, the more likely you are to find these imperfections. You can easily have a new piece of glass cut to fit, though, and this would have the advantage of being thinner and therefore lighter in weight; if you are brave enough, you can cut your own—my husband does mine for me.

Having got your old frame home, your first job is to get it clean. If it contains a picture and is backed, carefully cut away the brown paper which is glued over the back and then, with a small pointed pair of pliers, gently ease out the retaining pins that hold backing and picture in place. Often these will be rusty, and it is only too easy to break them or to spoil the wood in trying to get them out. (If the backing is thin wood or stiff card, or if the picture itself is mounted on stiff card, as old prints often are, this may serve very well as the mounting board for your own picture.)

Lift out the picture and the glass, and then give the frame a good brush, getting out as much dust and dirt as possible from all its ledges and corners. If it is solid wood you can then wash it carefully with soap and water: if it is veneered, painted or gilded, it must naturally be treated with greater delicacy, and gentle wiping with a cloth damped in water or paraffin may be all that is required, or all that it will stand. In any case, never let it get too wet, even if it is solid oak, or it may twist on drying, and the glue may be loosened (Scotch glue, used by many of the old framers, is soluble in water); if you bear this in mind, however, you should find that most dirty wooden frames will respond splendidly to careful scrubbing with a nailbrush and detergent. All traces of the detergent should then be rinsed away, and the wood carefully dried. If the washing has left the wood looking clean but rather dull, with the surface fibres slightly raised, try burnishing it all over with the back of a spoon.

If the glass is very grimy, wash it carefully in warm soapy water, dry it, and then polish it with a proprietary brand of glass cleaner, taking great care not to scratch it. Once it is clean, examine it carefully for scratches, bubbles and other blemishes. If it is good enough to use again, lay it aside carefully on sheets of clean newspaper (don't wrap it in fabric as it may pick up fluff and loose fibres, which might then be transferred to the mounting material of your picture).

You have now to put the picture into the frame. If the frame is a deep one—that is, if there is a quarter of an inch (six millimetres) or more of depth to take the glass, the picture and the backing—the procedure is straight-forward. Your biggest headache will be making sure that the inside of the glass is spotless, and the picture free from specks. More times than I care to remember, I have thoroughly cleaned the glass and brushed the velvet carefully with my damp toothbrush, only to find that when the velvet was securely behind the glass dozens of specks appeared from nowhere. Note, however, that unless your picture is absolutely flat, as might be the case with a composition using pressed petals and leaves, it will be necessary to leave some space between the picture and the glass, in order to leave room for the seeds and so on which stand proud of the picture's surface. The easiest way of doing this is to use a frame which has a "slip", and to reverse the usual positions of the slip and the glass. Usually the slip is inserted before the glass, so that it sits on top of it when viewed from the front, and the

Figure 11 This hawk, here seen larger than the actual picture, was inspired by a painting I saw: the image of a hawk design immediately took possession of me. His body is carried out in parsnip seeds and ash seed "wings", the latter being cleaned but not bleached; when I was working on the upper part of his wing, I used ash seed-cases with the seeds left in them, so that they were rather bulkier and gave, I hoped, the three-dimensional feeling of the shoulder. His eye is a black seed of honesty, his legs pieces of stem, and his perch a dried chrysanthemum stalk split to give it a more branch-like look. For his beak I used one of my favourite monkey puzzle spikes, trimming this slightly with a razor blade to get the proper grim curve. I was anxious here to create a portrait, rather than a stylized design or one of my more imaginary birds, so I tried to make it look as realistic as possible: an individual raptor, not a hawk motif. This was why I tried to get the three-dimensional effect and to portray sleeked-down crisp feathers, and why I did not use bleached materials – just the natural shaded browns and beiges.

Plates 9 and 10   I created these two pictures of the crane and the fish as companion pieces, mounted on my favourite black velvet in matching oak frames, and designed to tell a story. They were suggested by an Art Nouveau relief, but quickly developed a flavour of their own. I tried to copy Plate 9 later on, but couldn't recapture the crane's surprised expression as the fish popped up.

To make the cranes in these two pictures, I used hogweed and ash seed wings. I was particularly pleased by the discovery of a cornstalk whose knot was exactly right for the leg-joint of the triumphant crane in Plate 10. The fishes are made from the petals of everlasting flowers – one of the few occasions on which I have used flower petals – and the cranes' claws from willow leaf tips.

picture is pressed close to the glass; with a picture composed of pressed flowers, this can be a positive advantage. However, if your picture is created from, say, ash seed "wings" and hogweed seeds, you must have a space between the mount and the glass, and this is most easily achieved by inserting the glass first, so that it rests against the outer frame, then the slip, and *then* the picture, so that the depth of the slip is between the picture and the glass, providing for the slightly raised, three-dimensional effect so characteristic of these natural materials.

If the picture has an especially clustered and raised surface, the slip may not provide enough room. In that case, it may be necessary to make the slip deeper by gluing an additional strip of wood on the back of it, taking care to cut this extra piece so that it is narrower than the slip itself and will not be visible from the front. A coat of matt black paint will help to hide any strips of this kind; alternatively, you may cover them with a piece of the same fabric as you have used to mount the picture.

In extreme cases it may be necessary to build up the back of the frame to take the combined depths of glass, slip, three-dimensional picture, and back. This is most easily done by gluing in more strips of wood. The line drawing on the facing page shows a frame which has been built up in this way, to accommodate a fairly bulky seed picture.

When the picture is in position, resting tightly in place and absolutely secure —against the glass, if it is a flat picture, or against slip or wooden strips if it is raised—the back of the frame may be fixed in position. It is sometimes necessary to insert some sort of soft padding between the backing of the picture and the back of the frame; if, for example, you have an extra thickness at the corners and edges of the picture backing, where you have folded the mounting material over and stuck it down with Copydex, it may be wise to glue a little soft padding across the central area of the backing, to make a level surface which will fit snugly against the back board of the frame.

If, after all your efforts, the picture still does not fit as snugly and tightly as you would wish—and there should be absolutely no danger of its being shaken loose and shifting inside the frame—it may be necessary to pin it into place with small picture tacks or panel pins. If you decide to do this, however, do be careful not to bang harder than is absolutely essential, as the vibration may shake loose specks of dirt onto the mounting material, or, even worse, may fracture or dislodge part of the picture itself. For this reason it is better to screw the back board of the frame into place, rather than to pin it; and you should accordingly

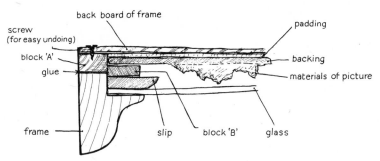

This diagram shows how a normal frame may be built up to accommodate an especially deep picture. If the backing of the picture were to rest on the slip, the materials of the picture would be squashed against the glass; therefore a strip of wood – block "B" – was inserted to provide the extra space. This meant that the back of the picture was proud of the original back of the frame, so the frame had to be built up all round – block "A" – and the back board screwed to these glued-on strips.

mark the position of the screws and prepare the screw holes *before* you put the picture into the frame.

It would, of course, be possible to glue the back board of the frame into place, but although this sounds an attractive solution, it makes it virtually impossible for you to get at the picture ever again, without risking damaging the frame and maybe the picture too. Accidents do happen—a seed, for instance, can be shaken loose—and it would be frustrating to find your first aid repairs hampered, even prevented altogether, by an irrevocable seal.

There is one final point to note before you begin. Decide in advance where you are going to put the fixings for the picture wire; mark the positions, measure up and make the screw holes *before* you actually insert the picture. If you try to do it afterwards, once picture and frame are safely assembled, you will again risk damaging the picture by the vibration, which would be heartbreaking.

Because a picture made in this way generally requires a deep frame, photo frames are rarely, if ever, any use. But there are exceptions to all rules, and if you are keen enough on a particular frame, it is often possible to devise a way of adapting it to hold your picture.

You may like to sign your picture. This is something I rarely do myself—how often does a signature contribute to the "rightness" of a picture?—but if you prefer to do so, there are various markers on sale which can be used on fabric, wood, and so on, or you can experiment with soft crayon, pastel, or dryish oil paint.

Figure 12   These Chinese cranes were conceived as companion pictures, and originally I had intended to make them identical, the one a mirror image of the other; as I worked at the designs, however, they gradually took on their own individuality, until they had achieved the poses which are shown here – the pair on the left suddenly gazing in some surprise, almost belligerence, while in the pair on the right, one is peaceably hunting for grubs and the other rears up as if to screech some comment. Nonetheless, I feel there is a satisfying balance between the two pictures.

When embarking on companion pictures of this kind, do check *before* you start that you have a really adequate supply of materials. Here I used very large hogweed seeds bleached by the wind and sun to a silvery tint, set off by the darkish olive of glycerined willow leaf tail-feathers. The eyes are lupin seeds; the claws thistle spikes; and the beaks dark brown monkey puzzle.

I mounted my cranes on my favourite black velvet, feeling that any other backing material would have detracted from the silvery-gold shimmer of the hogweed, but I provided a cool green border which seemed suitably Chinese and watery.

I have not yet tried decorating the frames themselves with seeds and leaves to echo and enhance those used in the picture; but this is something I do hope to try soon. Dust would obviously be a problem, and it would be alarmingly easy to damage the decorations, but I still think it might look very well, especially if one were not framing a picture at all but simply a mirror. If you mean to try it, you might find the note on wallpapering with leaves a help—this is on pages 119–20. One would obviously have to varnish the decorations. I think one would also need a stronger fixative than Copydex, particularly since the adhesive would have to be applied direct to wood, rather than to fabric whose fibres absorb the glue and thus help to grip seeds and leaves in place; Evostik might be well worth trying. This is an extension of the craft which seems to me to hold tremendous possibilities.

EXTENSIONS OF THE CRAFT

As I HAVE already said, there need be no limit to the work you can do with these materials, saving only the limit of your own imagination. In terms of size alone, I have found myself working on miniatures for lockets less than an inch across (under 25 mm) and on panels that were eight feet high by five feet wide ($2\frac{1}{2}$ metres by $1\frac{1}{2}$ metres). In spite of the enormous differences, the same basic rules apply. When working on miniatures, like the one shown in Figure 5 on page 78, I have found, as I mentioned earlier, that paper makes a more easily controlled backing than cotton or linen. This apart, it is merely a matter of steady hands, keen eyes and a good working light. And no draughts: even a sneeze can be disastrous!

A word of warning. Do be especially careful if you have to lift off a seed when working with paper as a backing. As I mentioned earlier, Copydex does not seep into and grip paper as it does fabric, so that when you try to lift away a seed it brings its dab of glue with it, and often that dab has stuck to others so that as you pull it drags along a whole stretch of dry Copydex, so dislodging all the rest of your work. If possible, cut the offending seed out with a sharp pair of scissors or

Figure 13 I created my Egyptian bird after I had been to the Tutankhamun Exhibition in London. He took shape very quickly – I generally find that, supposing the original idea translates readily into a sketch, the more static, formal, frieze-like images, such as this one, are fun to do, and very swift and easy; it is movement which causes the trouble, as it is more difficult to reduce to a simple outline. This bird was carried out in seeds and pampas grass, agreeably ruffled to offset the severe wing and tail, with the famous flat Egyptian frieze eye, pupilled with sunflower seed. His claws are made from artichoke spike and his beak from shaped monkey puzzle. The glittering seeds used in his body and wing came from Spain.

106

a scalpel and don't pull until you are quite sure it is free.

If you decide to mount your miniature on fabric, you may find velvet too bulky. It is hard, I think, to find a better mounting material than silk for small delicate pieces of work.

Jumping to the other extreme, the large panels, everything is magnified. The materials themselves can be much larger; on one occasion, for example, I used whole palm fronds bent into interesting curves and held in position with pins until the glue was dry. And whole ears of corn—wheat and barley especially— look splendid ranged in patterns. Preserved oak and beech leaves are a great standby, and come into their own with large pictures. Sycamore can be used to great advantage.

If you are using sycamore leaves, you may choose to try what I call an "open-work" technique. Their splendid autumn colouring apart, sycamore leaves have such an interesting outline that it seemed to me a pity not to show it off—yet the outline could not be seen clearly if the leaves were stuck down overlapping in the usual way; so I experimented, placing the leaves (each specimen as close to perfection as I could find) "in space", neither overlapped nor overlapping at all. Using this technique, it is possible, for example, to create the effect of a paisley pattern by ranging different leaves in swirls and whorls. I expect many people are familiar with the elaborate patterns of nails and screws and other goods with which old-fashioned ironmongers used sometimes to decorate their shop windows; the effect of some of my open-work designs, in retrospect, reminds me of these patterns, which used to fascinate me years ago when I was a child. There is, of course, no reason why this "open-work" technique should not be used in small pictures as well.

Large though the panels are, however, they are not the biggest job I have tackled. Having explored some of the possibilities—I hope not all—of natural materials in two-dimensional work, I ventured into the third dimension! The Dean and Chapter of St Paul's Cathedral, struck by the appropriateness of using

Plate 11 The Christmas Crib which I made for St Paul's Cathedral in London had to be conceived on a vast scale. The figures are larger than life-size (the close-up on page 112 shows the Kings in greater detail). The Crib was created entirely from the fruits of the earth. "*And the earth brought forth grass, and herb yielding seed after his kind, and the tree yielding fruit whose seed was in itself, after his kind . . . And God saw that it was good.*"

natural materials, commissioned me to create a Christmas Crib, larger than life-size. I had not attempted anything quite like this before, and had no precedent to guide me in the construction of the figures. The design was not so worrying—but having decided to create gigantic figures for the Crib, I had to find a way to make this practicable. The figures had to be strong, but also light, as they had to travel from the country to the Cathedral and would then have to be carried from the ground floor of the Cathedral up to the Whispering Gallery level, to be stored each year after their Christmas appearance.

I finally decided to make a very simple basic armature of wood, fixed to a wooden base, as shown in the drawing on the facing page. I then covered this with chicken wire, with a 1-inch mesh (25 mm), moulding it and pinching it and cutting it and stretching it until it was the shape I wanted the character to be. Very good effects can be got by pinching and squeezing the wire here and there until eventually one achieves a sense of "life".

I secured the chicken wire to the wooden armature with staples, and then covered the moulded wire with large strips of newspaper pasted on with wallpaper paste, which formed a smooth surface of *papier maché* on which to stick the leaves and reeds that were to "dress" the figures. Although the design was carefully modelled before I brought out my stock of leaves, seeds and so on, and although these materials were indeed simply the covering of the already-created figures, the whole design was conceived, at the very start, in terms of the natural materials whose surfaces would be thus presented to the world.

The problem of using these natural materials in three-dimensional rather than two-dimensional work really boils down to the difficulty of fixing leaves, seeds and so on securely to a curved and irregular surface instead of a flat one. I found that I had in some cases to abandon my faithful Copydex in favour of a stronger impact adhesive which held and stuck fast on contact (this was especially true when I had to fix relatively heavy materials to a vertical surface, as, for example, when I was sticking acorn or conker buttons down the front of a leafy coat!). Having chosen the materials I was going to use for each part of the figures—face, hair, robe, boots, cloak and so on—I then used two different techniques in sticking them to the *papier maché* surface. The leaves I gathered as they were turning brown and then pressed them for about a week and pasted them on exactly like scraps of wallpaper, using ordinary wallpaper paste—Polycell; when they had dried out, I sprayed them with a polyurethane varnish to preserve and protect them. As for the bulkier materials, such as reeds and pods, I glued them

110

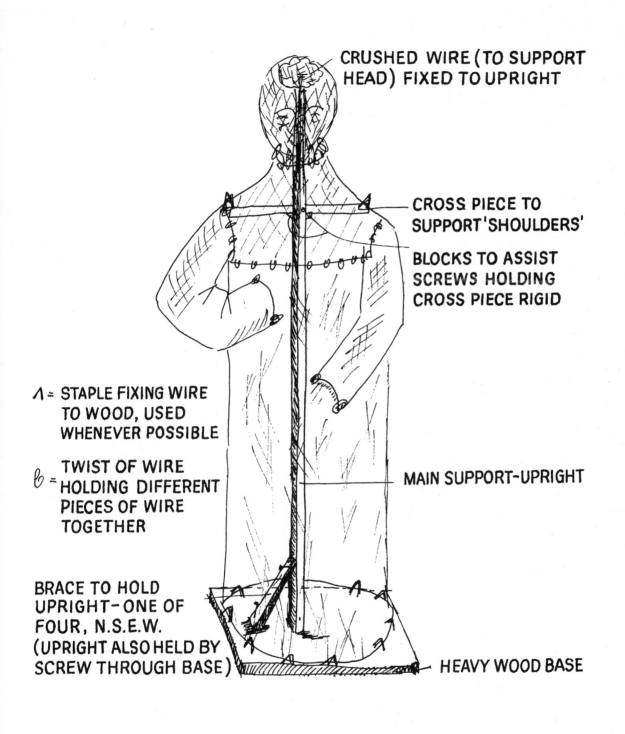

CRUSHED WIRE (TO SUPPORT HEAD) FIXED TO UPRIGHT

CROSS PIECE TO SUPPORT 'SHOULDERS'

BLOCKS TO ASSIST SCREWS HOLDING CROSS PIECE RIGID

∧ = STAPLE FIXING WIRE TO WOOD, USED WHENEVER POSSIBLE

ℓ = TWIST OF WIRE HOLDING DIFFERENT PIECES OF WIRE TOGETHER

MAIN SUPPORT-UPRIGHT

BRACE TO HOLD UPRIGHT-ONE OF FOUR, N.S.E.W. (UPRIGHT ALSO HELD BY SCREW THROUGH BASE)

HEAVY WOOD BASE

Plate 12   A close-up view of the Crib figures.

into position with a very strong glue—Evostik—and again varnished them, just as I had done with the leaves.

I used as many different materials as I could find, so that I could get as much variation of texture and colour as possible. I used bark for some faces (Joseph's for example), leaves for others (Mary's face is of sycamore leaves), thistles for the faces of the First and Third Shepherds, elm seeds for the Second; common reed to line two of the Shepherds' coats and for the cloak of the third, and to create the aristocratic Afghan Hound that attends the Three Kings; elephant grass for the Sheep, and pampas grass plumes for the Lamb; Mary is dressed in black-currant leaves decorated with delphinium seed pods, Joseph in aralia leaves; the First King is cloaked in mulberry leaves and robed in common reeds decorated with palm leaves and thistle, the Second is robed in walnut leaves and corn, the Third in beech leaves and beech nuts under a sycamore leaf cloak; the First Shepherd wears a cloak of agave (the skeleton of cacti), the Second has hair of lupin pods, the Third is booted in elm leaves; and the Infant Jesus is swaddled in bleached grass and honesty. For the Angels—there are six, the largest being twenty-five feet long (over eight metres)—I used honesty, pampas grass, and thousands and thousands of bleached aspidistra leaves. I used corn for crowns, leaves for wings, reeds for the Ass and oak leaves for the Ox. Celebrating the birth of Christ with the fruits of the earth indeed!

CHILDREN AND THE CRAFT

MY CHILDREN'S EARLY enthusiasm—born no doubt of the delights of kicking through heaps of leaves in the Park—fairly soon gave way to a feeling that seeds and leaves were just one big bore. They thought I was getting rather odd, forever on the look-out for new material, prowling through friends' gardens, and even crouching in the street to retrieve a potentially valuable something from hedge or pavement.

But when the pictures began to appear, their attitude changed once more. Looking at the finished article, they began to understand what it was all about, and they became fired in their turn with a desire to carry out similar work; they began to copy me, making pictures of their own, some of which are illustrated here.

At first, I must admit, I gave them some of my less valuable materials solely to keep them quiet. Much as I adore my children, I do find it absolutely impossible to get any work done when they are breathing down my neck or crouching under my elbow saying—however tentatively—"Can I do that?" or "Can I have one of those?" or "What's that leaf from?"

So one day I spread newspaper on a table, gave them a tube of Copydex and an assortment of the larger materials that they could handle easily without the help of tweezers, and left them to get on with it. Half an hour of peace followed. Then, once again, I was aware of my son hovering at my elbow. Well, I'd had half an hour, and was quite a bit further on with my work, so I was fairly resigned to resuming the role of Mother when I turned to see what he wanted. He was standing there shyly, but obviously as pleased as Punch, holding the most delightful picture of a little bird. All his own work, and not in any way a copy of any of mine. You can imagine how thrilled I was. My son was seven at this time. My daughter, who is younger, rushed in seconds later, red-faced with enthusiasm, clutching a rather gummy picture of a tree, laboured over with real

Figure 14 Goose by Ben Frow, aged 9 – he used untreated ash seed-cases, with the seeds still inside, reversed to give bulk.

love and determination—just as entrancing in its way as the bird, if only for her parents!

That my son should turn in an interesting picture did not really surprise me (he had shown some signs of early skill before) so much as the fact that he seemed to have no difficulty in handling the materials or understanding the basic technique. I realized a little later that he had already had considerable practice in making collage pictures at his primary school, where they used not seeds and leaves but such exciting and cheap and readily available materials as rice, cornflakes, and spaghetti! What was new to him, and what fascinated him from the first, was the way individual seeds and leaves resembled actual parts of animals, par-

Figure 15 Tree by Josephine Frow, aged 7: in elm seeds and cornstalks.

ticularly birds. Claws, beaks, feathers—he had the knack of seeing them ready-formed in the materials, and of assembling them in such a way that the rest of us could see them too. Figure 14 on page 115 shows a goose which he made when he was nine.

This knack, this freshness of approach, is of course something that all children have in some degree, and is one of the things that make natural materials such a good medium for children to use.

There is, of course, no reason why children's pictures, any more than adults', should be realistic. The materials lend themselves very well to abstracts and to pattern-making. Indeed, my daughter early on developed her own style, quite different from her brother's, and made some very pretty pictures and patterns using split peas and rice along with the seeds and leaves. One of her most successful attempts was a large plane leaf decorated all over with smaller materials.

116

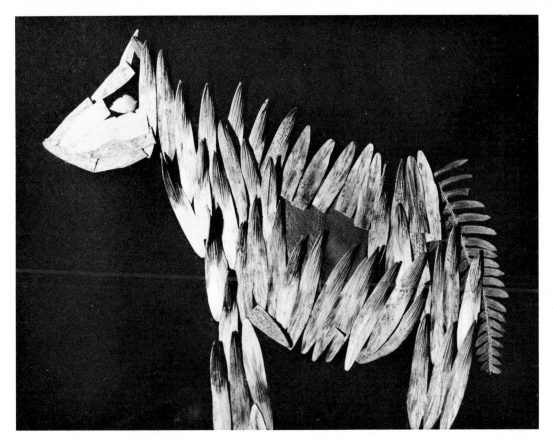

Figure 16 Horse, in ash seeds and bracken: Ben Frow, aged 7.

These materials are also particularly good for children to use because they encourage them to look at the environment very closely, to learn about plants, to examine seeds. I believe that the close examination of seeds and leaves and plants can only increase a sense of wonder and delight in the natural world we live in—surely vitally important now, at a time when we are so greatly concerned over the conservation of the environment.

But there are other, perhaps more immediately practical, considerations. While expeditions to collect materials can be as much fun in their way as actually putting the materials to use, there are aspects which give this medium the edge over many others as far as children are concerned. For children who have lively imaginations but who "cannot draw", and so are inhibited from trying to express themselves in pictures, the ready-made aspect of these materials is heaven-sent. For in making a picture or a design or a collage from natural

Figure 17   Bird, in ash and hogweed: Katie Copplestone, aged 10.

materials, it is the relation of one piece to another that is important, the ability and the imagination to see that by altering the angle of, say, a bird's willow leaf beak you can change his mood from one of misery to one of elation; the faculty of making sense of a pencil outline, while useful, is not by any manner of means essential or of vital importance.

And to end with, one should perhaps mention the most down-to-earth and practical point of all: these wonderful materials, beautiful, subtle, intricate, renewed every year but always different, always unique, will cost you absolutely nothing.

APPENDIX
A NOTE ON WALLPAPERING WITH LEAVES

USING LEAVES FOR decorating walls can be very exciting. Nearly every kind of leaf *can* be used but tree and shrub leaves are best as their texture is generally tougher; moreover, if you wait until they turn colour in the autumn, you can get a wonderful variety of shades.

First you must collect your leaves! This is very different from collecting your picture "palette", since with pictures you may only need a handful of any one kind of leaf to gain your effect, but for decorating a wall you will need hundreds —the wall always seems to be just that much larger than you anticipated when you began.

The moment to collect your autumn leaves is just when they have turned brown or golden and fallen to the earth. If you can go collecting just after a shower of rain—*not* a downpour—and gather them while they are still moist, so much the better. If not, put them into large bowls as soon as you get home and pour boiling water over them to keep them supple. Leave them for twenty-four hours, then fish them out of the water and press them between sheets of newspaper under bricks for a further twenty-four hours; then they will be ready for you to start work.

The leaves I have used most have been plane, sycamore, walnut, elm and mulberry. Plane leaves are like great golden fans; they may need pressing a little longer than the others as they are the toughest of all—they *must* lie completely flat before you start decorating. Mulberry leaves are very beautiful and delicate and turn a lovely pale gold colour, but they are not as tough as other leaves *and will not need to be soaked in water beforehand*—just press them.

Before applying the leaves, paint the wall whatever colour you think will make the best background. I have found white the most successful, but this is something which it is up to you to decide. Use a flat emulsion paint, and make sure it dries thoroughly before you go on.

To apply the leaves, you use exactly the same method as if you were pasting up ordinary wallpaper. Mix a normal solution of wallpaper paste—I have found Polycell best—and then apply this to the *smooth* side of the leaf; if you try pasting it on the other side, the raised veins will prevent the leaf from sticking flat against the wall. Now simply stick your leaf onto the painted surface. It is entirely up to you what design you follow—if any; you can make formal patterns, with the leaves in vertical lines, or abstract clusters, or have leaves tip to tip with the paint as a backing, or create vast overlapping swirls.

It will take quite a time to cover the wall—longer than you think when you begin. I have found it best to do a little each day. You can get such wonderful effects with this three-dimensional wallpaper—for that is exactly what it looks like when you have finished—that it is well worth the time and effort.

When you have covered the whole wall, allow the leaves to dry out thoroughly. Then spray the wall with a polyurethane varnish—this will seal the leaves, and give the "paper" a slightly glossy effect.

As long as you varnish it well, there is no reason why you should not wash the wall down if it gets dirty; but don't use a hard abrasive or you may remove the varnish as well as the dirt, and all your hard work will be wasted!

INDEX

by Lilian Rubin

Note: an asterisk denotes an illustration; when a leaf, seed or plant is portrayed in a special line drawing, the page reference is asterisked and given in bold type; when, however, leaves, seeds or other natural plant material have been used in the creation of one of the author's pictures, the page reference for that picture is asterisked and given in Roman type and is cross-referenced under the relevant materials. Picture titles are also given in bold type.

126